Cram101 Textbook Outlines to accompany:

Essentials of Organizational Behavior

Robbins, 8th Edition

An Academic Internet Publishers (AIPI) publication (c) 2007.

You have a discounted membership at www.Cram101.com with this book.

Get all of the practice tests for the chapters of this textbook, and access in-depth reference material for writing essays and papers. Here is an example from a Cram101 Biology text:

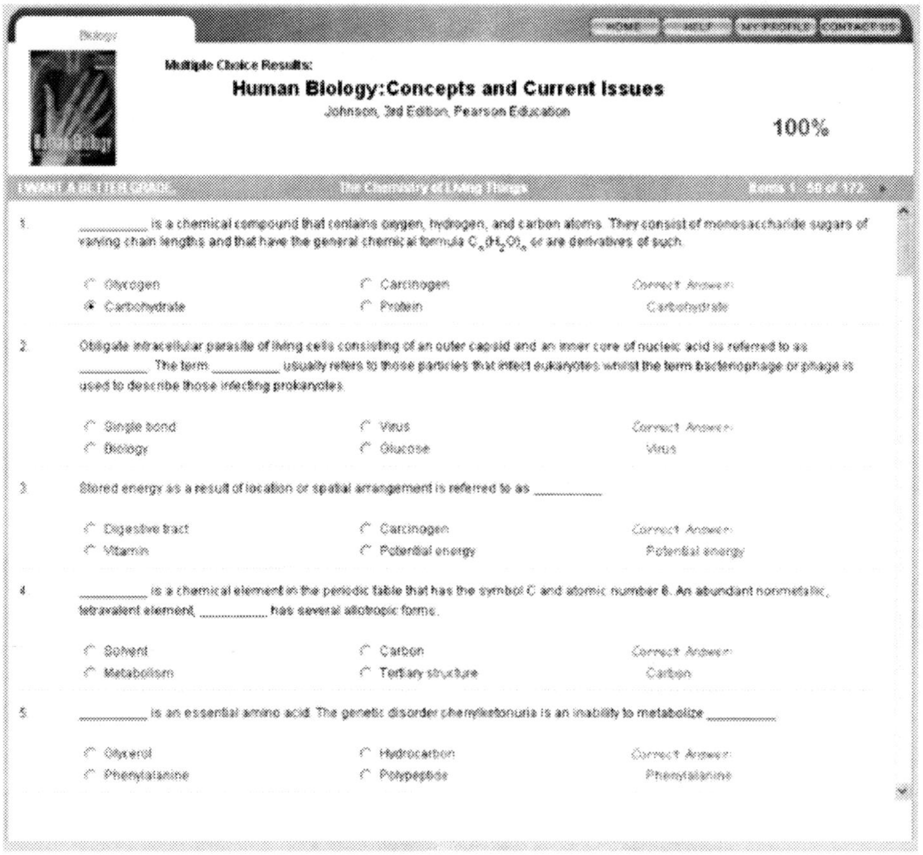

When you need problem solving help with math, stats, and other disciplines, www.Cram101.com will walk through the formulas and solutions step by step.

With Cram101.com online, you also have access to extensive reference material.

You will nail those essays and papers. Here is an example from a Cram101 Biology text:

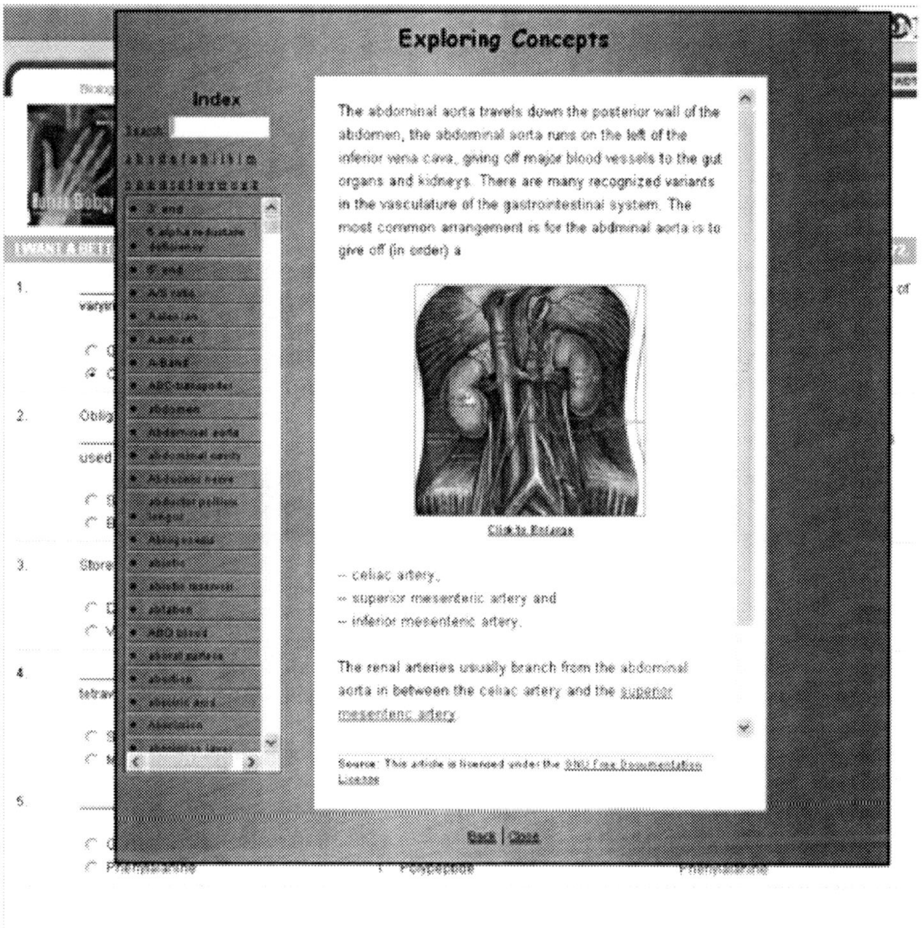

Visit **www.Cram101.com**, click Sign Up at the top of the screen, and enter DK73DW in the promo code box on the registration screen. Access to www.Cram101.com is normally $9.95, but because you have purchased this book, your access fee is only $4.95. Sign up and stop highlighting textbooks forever.

Learning System

Cram101 Textbook Outlines is a learning system. The notes in this book are the highlights of your textbook, you will never have to highlight a book again.

How to use this book. Take this book to class, it is your notebook for the lecture. The notes and highlights on the left hand side of the pages follow the outline and order of the textbook. All you have to do is follow along while your intructor presents the lecture. Circle the items emphasized in class and add other important information on the right side. With Cram101 Textbook Outlines you'll spend less time writing and more time listening. Learning becomes more efficient.

Cram101.com Online

Increase your studying efficiency by using Cram101.com's practice tests and online reference material. It is the perfect complement to Cram101 Textbook Outlines. Use self-teaching matching tests or simulate in-class testing with comprehensive multiple choice tests, or simply use Cram's true and false tests for quick review. Cram101.com even allows you to enter your in-class notes for an integrated studying format combining the textbook notes with your class notes.

Visit **www.Cram101.com**, click Sign Up at the top of the screen, and enter **DK73DW2928** in the promo code box on the registration screen. Access to www.Cram101.com is normally $9.95, but because you have purchased this book, your access fee is only $4.95. Sign up and stop highlighting textbooks forever.

 ISBN: 1-4288-1157-5

Essentials of Organizational Behavior
Robbins, 8th

CONTENTS

Accounting	A system that collects and processes financial information about an organization and reports that information to decision makers is referred to as accounting.
Management	Management characterizes the process of leading and directing all or part of an organization, often a business, through the deployment and manipulation of resources. Early twentieth-century management writer Mary Parker Follett defined management as "the art of getting things done through people."
Economics	The social science dealing with the use of scarce resources to obtain the maximum satisfaction of society's virtually unlimited economic wants is an economics.
Organizational Behavior	The study of human behavior in organizational settings, the interface between human behavior and the organization, and the organization itself is called organizational behavior.
Productivity	Productivity refers to the total output of goods and services in a given period of time divided by work hours.
Turnover	Turnover in a financial context refers to the rate at which a provider of goods cycles through its average inventory. Turnover in a human resources context refers to the characteristic of a given company or industry, relative to rate at which an employer gains and loses staff.
Organizational citizenship	The extent to which a person's behavior makes a positive overall contribution to the organization is referred to as organizational citizenship.
Job satisfaction	Job satisfaction describes how content an individual is with his or her job. It is a relatively recent term since in previous centuries the jobs available to a particular person were often predetermined by the occupation of that person's parent.
Contribution	In business organization law, the cash or property contributed to a business by its owners is referred to as contribution.
Leadership	Management merely consists of leadership applied to business situations; or in other words: management forms a sub-set of the broader process of leadership.
Performance appraisal	An evaluation in which the performance level of employees is measured against established standards to make decisions about promotions, compenzation, additional training, or firing is referred to as performance appraisal.
Workforce diversity	The similarities and differences in such characteristics as age, gender, ethnic heritage, physical abilities and disabilities, race, and sexual orientation among the employees of organizations is called workforce diversity.
Organizational culture	The mindset of employees, including their shared beliefs, values, and goals is called the organizational culture.
Group dynamics	The term group dynamics implies that individual behaviors may differ depending on individuals' current or prospective connections to a sociological group. Group dynamics is the field of study within the social sciences that focuses on the nature of groups. Urges to belong or to identify may make for distinctly different attitudes (recognized or unrecognized), and the influence of a group may rapidly become strong, influencing or overwhelming individual proclivities and actions.
Bureaucracy	Bureaucracy refers to an organization with many layers of managers who set rules and regulations and oversee all decisions.
Balance	In banking and accountancy, the outstanding balance is the amount of money owned, (or due), that remains in a deposit account (or a loan account) at a given date, after all past remittances, payments and withdrawal have been accounted for. It can be positive (then, in the balance sheet of a firm, it is an asset) or negative (a liability).
Formal organization	Formal organization refers to the structure that details lines of responsibility, authority, and position; that is, the structure shown on organization charts.

Distribution	Distribution in economics, the manner in which total output and income is distributed among individuals or factors.
Organizational environment	Organizational environment refers to everything outside an organization. It includes all elements, people, other organizations, economic factors, objects, and events that lie outside the boundaries of the organization.
Technology	The body of knowledge and techniques that can be used to combine economic resources to produce goods and services is called technology.
Globalization	The increasing world-wide integration of markets for goods, services and capital that attracted special attention in the late 1990s is called globalization.
Firm	An organization that employs resources to produce a good or service for profit and owns and operates one or more plants is referred to as a firm.
ExxonMobil	ExxonMobil is the largest publicly traded integrated oil and gas company in the world, formed on November 30, 1999, by the merger of Exxon and Mobil. It is the sixth-largest company in the world as ranked by the Forbes Global 2000 and the largest company in the world (by revenue) as ranked by the Fortune Global 500.
Revenue	Revenue is a U.S. business term for the amount of money that a company receives from its activities, mostly from sales of products and/or services to customers.
Developing country	Developing country refers to a country whose per capita income is low by world standards. Same as LDC. As usually used, it does not necessarily connote that the country's income is rising.
Nokia	Nokia Corporation is the world's largest manufacturer of mobile telephones (as of June 2006), with a global market share of approximately 34% in Q2 of 2006. It produces mobile phones for every major market and protocol, including GSM, CDMA, and W-CDMA (UMTS).
Assignment	A transfer of property or some right or interest is referred to as assignment.
Subsidiary	A company that is controlled by another company or corporation is a subsidiary.
Capitalism	Capitalism refers to an economic system in which capital is mostly owned by private individuals and corporations. Contrasts with communism.
Profit	Profit refers to the return to the resource entrepreneurial ability; total revenue minus total cost.
Disney	Disney is one of the largest media and entertainment corporations in the world. Founded on October 16, 1923 by brothers Walt and Roy Disney as a small animation studio, today it is one of the largest Hollywood studios and also owns nine theme parks and several television networks, including the American Broadcasting Company (ABC).
Minimum wage	The lowest wage employers may legally pay for an hour of work is the minimum wage.
Labor	People's physical and mental talents and efforts that are used to help produce goods and services are called labor.
Wage	The payment for the service of a unit of labor, per unit time. In trade theory, it is the only payment to labor, usually unskilled labor. In empirical work, wage data may exclude other compenzation, which must be added to get the total cost of employment.
Economy	The income, expenditures, and resources that affect the cost of running a business and household are called an economy.
Comparative advantage	The ability to produce a good at lower cost, relative to other goods, compared to another country is a comparative advantage.
Competitiveness	Competitiveness usually refers to characteristics that permit a firm to compete effectively with other firms due to low cost or superior technology, perhaps internationally.

Interest	In finance and economics, interest is the price paid by a borrower for the use of a lender's money. In other words, interest is the amount of paid to "rent" money for a period of time.
Policy	Similar to a script in that a policy can be a less than completely rational decision-making method. Involves the use of a pre-existing set of decision steps for any problem that presents itself.
Accommodation	Accommodation is a term used to describe a delivery of nonconforming goods meant as a partial performance of a contract for the sale of goods, where a full performance is not possible.
Domestic	From or in one's own country. A domestic producer is one that produces inside the home country. A domestic price is the price inside the home country. Opposite of 'foreign' or 'world.'.
Adverse impact	Adverse impact refers to the rejection for employment, placement, or promotion of a significantly higher percentage of a protected class, when compared with a non-protected class.
Customs	Customs is an authority or agency in a country responsible for collecting customs duties and for controlling the flow of people, animals and goods (including personal effects and hazardous items) in and out of the country.
Holding	The holding is a court's determination of a matter of law based on the issue presented in the particular case. In other words: under this law, with these facts, this result.
Labor force	In economics the labor force is the group of people who have a potential for being employed.
Demographic	A demographic is a term used in marketing and broadcasting, to describe a demographic grouping or a market segment.
Applicant	In many tribunal and administrative law suits, the person who initiates the claim is called the applicant.
Composition	An out-of-court settlement in which creditors agree to accept a fractional settlement on their original claim is referred to as composition.
Diversity training	Diversity training refers to training designed to change employee attitudes about diversity and/or develop skills needed to work with a diverse workforce.
Innovation	Innovation refers to the first commercially successful introduction of a new product, the use of a new method of production, or the creation of a new form of business organization.
Service	Service refers to a “non tangible product” that is not embodied in a physical good and that typically effects some change in another product, person, or institution. Contrasts with good.
Excess supply	Supply minus demand. Thus a country's supply of exports of a homogeneous good is its excess supply of that good.
Industry	A group of firms that produce identical or similar products is an industry. It is also used specifically to refer to an area of economic production focused on manufacturing which involves large amounts of capital investment before any profit can be realized, also called "heavy industry".
Supply	Supply is the aggregate amount of any material good that can be called into being at a certain price point; it comprises one half of the equation of supply and demand. In classical economic theory, a curve representing supply is one of the factors that produce price.
Excess capacity	Excess capacity refers to plant resources that are underused when imperfectly competitive firms produce less output than that associated with purely competitive firms, who by definiation, are achieving minimum average total cost.
Quality management	Quality management is a method for ensuring that all the activities necessary to design, develop and implement a product or service are effective and efficient with respect to the system and its performance.
Reengineering	The fundamental rethinking and redesign of business processes to achieve improvements in critical

	measures of performance, such as cost, quality, service, speed, and customer satisfaction is referred to as reengineering.
Process reengineering	Process reengineering refers to the total rethinking and redesign of organizational process to improve performance and innovation; involves analyzing, streamlining, and reconfiguring actions and tasks to achieve work goals.
Internal customer	An individuals or unit within the firm that receives services from other entities within the organization is an internal customer.
Accounts payable	A written record of all vendors to whom the business firm owes money is referred to as accounts payable.
Personnel	A collective term for all of the employees of an organization. Personnel is also commonly used to refer to the personnel management function or the organizational unit responsible for administering personnel programs.
Complaint	The pleading in a civil case in which the plaintiff states his claim and requests relief is called complaint. In the common law, it is a formal legal document that sets out the basic facts and legal reasons that the filing party (the plaintiffs) believes are sufficient to support a claim against another person, persons, entity or entities (the defendants) that entitles the plaintiff(s) to a remedy (either money damages or injunctive relief).
Operation	A standardized method or technique that is performed repetitively, often on different materials resulting in different finished goods is called an operation.
Variable	A variable is something measured by a number; it is used to analyze what happens to other things when the size of that number changes.
Empowerment	Giving employees the authority and responsibility to respond quickly to customer requests is called empowerment.
Gain	In finance, gain is a profit or an increase in value of an investment such as a stock or bond. Gain is calculated by fair market value or the proceeds from the sale of the investment minus the sum of the purchase price and all costs associated with it.
Customer service	The ability of logistics management to satisfy users in terms of time, dependability, communication, and convenience is called the customer service.
Developed country	A developed country is one that enjoys a relatively high standard of living derived through an industrialized, diversified economy. Countries with a very high Human Development Index are generally considered developed countries.
Customer satisfaction	Customer satisfaction is a business term which is used to capture the idea of measuring how satisfied an enterprise's customers are with the organization's efforts in a marketplace.
Telecommuting	Telecommuting is a work arrangement in which employees enjoy limited flexibility in working location and hours.
Aid	Assistance provided by countries and by international institutions such as the World Bank to developing countries in the form of monetary grants, loans at low interest rates, in kind, or a combination of these is called aid. Aid can also refer to assistance of any type rendered to benefit some group or individual.
Pension	A pension is a steady income given to a person (usually after retirement). Pensions are typically payments made in the form of a guaranteed annuity to a retired or disabled employee.
Security	Security refers to a claim on the borrower future income that is sold by the borrower to the lender. A security is a type of transferable interest representing financial value.
DaimlerChrysler	In 2002, the merged company, DaimlerChrysler, appeared to run two independent product lines, with few

	signs of corporate integration. In 2003, however, it was alleged by the Detroit News that the "merger of equals" was, in fact, a takeover.
Loyalty	Marketers tend to define customer loyalty as making repeat purchases. Some argue that it should be defined attitudinally as a strongly positive feeling about the brand.
Devise	In a will, a gift of real property is called a devise.
Administrator	Administrator refers to the personal representative appointed by a probate court to settle the estate of a deceased person who died.
Expense	In accounting, an expense represents an event in which an asset is used up or a liability is incurred. In terms of the accounting equation, expenses reduce owners' equity.
Oath	Any form of attestation by which a person signifies that he is bound in conscience to perform an act faithfully and truthfully is referred to as oath.

Capital	Capital generally refers to financial wealth, especially that used to start or maintain a business. In classical economics, capital is one of four factors of production, the others being land and labor and entrepreneurship.
Converse	Converse is an American shoe company which has been making shoes since the early 20th century. The company's main turning point came in 1917 when the Converse All-Star basketball shoe was introduced. This was a real innovation at the time, considering the sport was only 25 years old.
Value system	A value system refers to how an individual or a group of individuals organize their ethical or ideological values. A well-defined value system is a moral code.
Terminal value	In finance, the terminal value of a security is the present value at a future point in time of all future cash flows. It is most often used in multi-stage discounted cash flow analysis, and allows for the limitation of cash flow projections to a several-year period.
Instrumental value	A values that reflects a person's beliefs about the means for achieving desired ends is referred to as an instrumental value.
Union	A worker association that bargains with employers over wages and working conditions is called a union.
Preference	The act of a debtor in paying or securing one or more of his creditors in a manner more favorable to them than to other creditors or to the exclusion of such other creditors is a preference. In the absence of statute, a preference is perfectly good, but to be legal it must be bona fide, and not a mere subterfuge of the debtor to secure a future benefit to himself or to prevent the application of his property to his debts.
Corporation	A legal entity chartered by a state or the Federal government that is distinct and separate from the individuals who own it is a corporation. This separation gives the corporation unique powers which other legal entities lack.
Interest	In finance and economics, interest is the price paid by a borrower for the use of a lender's money. In other words, interest is the amount of paid to "rent" money for a period of time.
Great Depression	The period of severe economic contraction and high unemployment that began in 1929 and continued throughout the 1930s is referred to as the Great Depression.
Depression	Depression refers to a prolonged period characterized by high unemployment, low output and investment, depressed business confidence, falling prices, and widespread business failures. A milder form of business downturn is a recession.
Status quo	Status quo is a Latin term meaning the present, current, existing state of affairs.
Authority	Authority in agency law, refers to an agent's ability to affect his principal's legal relations with third parties. Also used to refer to an actor's legal power or ability to do something. In addition, sometimes used to refer to a statute, case, or other legal source that justifies a particular result.
Security	Security refers to a claim on the borrower future income that is sold by the borrower to the lender. A security is a type of transferable interest representing financial value.
Globalization	The increasing world-wide integration of markets for goods, services and capital that attracted special attention in the late 1990s is called globalization.
Aid	Assistance provided by countries and by international institutions such as the World Bank to developing countries in the form of monetary grants, loans at low interest rates, in kind, or a combination of these is called aid. Aid can also refer to assistance of any type rendered to benefit some group or individual.
Balance	In banking and accountancy, the outstanding balance is the amount of money owned, (or due),

	that remains in a deposit account (or a loan account) at a given date, after all past remittances, payments and withdrawal have been accounted for. It can be positive (then, in the balance sheet of a firm, it is an asset) or negative (a liability).
Economy	The income, expenditures, and resources that affect the cost of running a business and household are called an economy.
Technology	The body of knowledge and techniques that can be used to combine economic resources to produce goods and services is called technology.
Teamwork	That which occurs when group members work together in ways that utilize their skills well to accomplish a purpose is called teamwork.
Accounting	A system that collects and processes financial information about an organization and reports that information to decision makers is referred to as accounting.
Management	Management characterizes the process of leading and directing all or part of an organization, often a business, through the deployment and manipulation of resources. Early twentieth-century management writer Mary Parker Follett defined management as "the art of getting things done through people."
Loyalty	Marketers tend to define customer loyalty as making repeat purchases. Some argue that it should be defined attitudinally as a strongly positive feeling about the brand.
Ethical dilemma	An ethical dilemma is a situation that often involves an apparent conflict between moral imperatives, in which to obey one would result in transgressing another.
Power distance	Power distance refers to the degree to which the less powerful members of society expect there to be differences in the levels of power. A high score suggests that there is an expectation that some individuals wield larger amounts of power than others. Countries with high power distance rating are often characterized by a high rate of political violence.
Collectivism	Collectivism is a term used to describe that things should be owned by the group and used for the benefit of all rather than being owned by individuals.
Acquisition	A company's purchase of the property and obligations of another company is an acquisition.
Welfare	Welfare refers to the economic well being of an individual, group, or economy. For individuals, it is conceptualized by a utility function. For groups, including countries and the world, it is a tricky philosophical concept, since individuals fare differently.
Uncertainty avoidance	The extent to which people prefer to be in clear and unambiguous situations is referred to as the uncertainty avoidance.
Assessment	Collecting information and providing feedback to employees about their behavior, communication style, or skills is an assessment.
Organizational Behavior	The study of human behavior in organizational settings, the interface between human behavior and the organization, and the organization itself is called organizational behavior.
Leadership	Management merely consists of leadership applied to business situations; or in other words: management forms a sub-set of the broader process of leadership.
Tender	An unconditional offer of payment, consisting in the actual production in money or legal tender of a sum not less than the amount due.
Domestic	From or in one's own country. A domestic producer is one that produces inside the home country. A domestic price is the price inside the home country. Opposite of 'foreign' or 'world.'.
Context	The effect of the background under which a message often takes on more and richer meaning is a context. Context is especially important in cross-cultural interactions because some

	cultures are said to be high context or low context.
Cultural values	The values that employees need to have and act on for the organization to act on the strategic values are called cultural values.
Job satisfaction	Job satisfaction describes how content an individual is with his or her job. It is a relatively recent term since in previous centuries the jobs available to a particular person were often predetermined by the occupation of that person's parent.
Promotion	Promotion refers to all the techniques sellers use to motivate people to buy products or services. An attempt by marketers to inform people about products and to persuade them to participate in an exchange.
Policy	Similar to a script in that a policy can be a less than completely rational decision-making method. Involves the use of a pre-existing set of decision steps for any problem that presents itself.
Productivity	Productivity refers to the total output of goods and services in a given period of time divided by work hours.
Variable	A variable is something measured by a number; it is used to analyze what happens to other things when the size of that number changes.
Comprehensive	A comprehensive refers to a layout accurate in size, color, scheme, and other necessary details to show how a final ad will look. For presentation only, never for reproduction.
Supervisor	A Supervisor is an employee of an organization with some of the powers and responsibilities of management, occupying a role between true manager and a regular employee. A Supervisor position is typically the first step towards being promoted into a management role.
Cognitive dissonance	The anxiety a person experiences when he or she simultaneously possesses two sets of knowledge or perceptions that are contradictory or incongruent is referred to as the cognitive dissonance.
Balance sheet	A statement of the assets, liabilities, and net worth of a firm or individual at some given time often at the end of its "fiscal year," is referred to as a balance sheet.
Service	Service refers to a "non tangible product" that is not embodied in a physical good and that typically effects some change in another product, person, or institution. Contrasts with good.
Evaluation	The consumer's appraisal of the product or brand on important attributes is called evaluation.
Consideration	Consideration in contract law, a basic requirement for an enforceable agreement under traditional contract principles, defined in this text as legal value, bargained for and given in exchange for an act or promise. In corporation law, cash or property contributed to a corporation in exchange for shares, or a promise to contribute such cash or property.
Specificity	The property that a policy measure applies to one or a group of enterprises or industries, as opposed to all industries, is called specificity.
Attribution	Under certain circumstances, the tax law applies attribution rules to assign to one taxpayer the ownership interest of another taxpayer.
Attribution theory	Attribution theory suggests that we attribute causes to behavior based on observations of certain characteristics of that behavior. Employees observe their own behavior, determine whether it is a response to external or internal factors, and shape their future motivated behavior accordingly.
External	Attributing the cause of work behavior to some reason that is external to the person is

attribution	referred to as external attribution.
Halo effect	A halo effect is one where the perceived positive features of a particular item extend to a broader brand.
Marketing research	Marketing research refers to the analysis of markets to determine opportunities and challenges, and to find the information needed to make good decisions.
Marketing	Promoting and selling products or services to customers, or prospective customers, is referred to as marketing.
Mistake	In contract law a mistake is incorrect understanding by one or more parties to a contract and may be used as grounds to invalidate the agreement. Common law has identified three different types of mistake in contract: unilateral mistake, mutual mistake, and common mistake.
Instrument	Instrument refers to an economic variable that is controlled by policy makers and can be used to influence other variables, called targets. Examples are monetary and fiscal policies used to achieve external and internal balance.
Trial	An examination before a competent tribunal, according to the law of the land, of the facts or law put in issue in a cause, for the purpose of determining such issue is a trial. When the court hears and determines any issue of fact or law for the purpose of determining the rights of the parties, it may be considered a trial.
Applicant	In many tribunal and administrative law suits, the person who initiates the claim is called the applicant.
Allocate	Allocate refers to the assignment of income for various tax purposes. A multistate corporation's nonbusiness income usually is distributed to the state where the nonbusiness assets are located; it is not apportioned with the rest of the entity's income.
Turnover	Turnover in a financial context refers to the rate at which a provider of goods cycles through its average inventory. Turnover in a human resources context refers to the characteristic of a given company or industry, relative to rate at which an employer gains and loses staff.
Wage	The payment for the service of a unit of labor, per unit time. In trade theory, it is the only payment to labor, usually unskilled labor. In empirical work, wage data may exclude other compenzation, which must be added to get the total cost of employment.
Distortion	Distortion refers to any departure from the ideal of perfect competition that interferes with economic agents maximizing social welfare when they maximize their own.

Organizational Behavior	The study of human behavior in organizational settings, the interface between human behavior and the organization, and the organization itself is called organizational behavior.
Categorizing	The act of placing strengths and weaknesses into categories in generic internal assessment is called categorizing.
Personality test	A personality test aims to describe aspects of a person's character that remain stable throughout a person's lifetime. A model of personality were first posited by Greek philosopher/physician Hippocrates.
Apple Computer	Apple Computer has been a major player in the evolution of personal computing since its founding in 1976. The Apple II microcomputer, introduced in 1977, was a hit with home users.
Microsoft	Microsoft is a multinational computer technology corporation with 2004 global annual sales of US$39.79 billion and 71,553 employees in 102 countries and regions as of July 2006. It develops, manufactures, licenses, and supports a wide range of software products for computing devices.
Honda	With more than 14 million internal combustion engines built each year, Honda is the largest engine-maker in the world. In 2004, the company began to produce diesel motors, which were both very quiet whilst not requiring particulate filters to pass pollution standards. It is arguable, however, that the foundation of their success is the motorcycle division.
Firm	An organization that employs resources to produce a good or service for profit and owns and operates one or more plants is referred to as a firm.
Sony	Sony is a multinational corporation and one of the world's largest media conglomerates founded in Tokyo, Japan. One of its divisions Sony Electronics is one of the leading manufacturers of electronics, video, communications, and information technology products for the consumer and professional markets.
Cooperative	A business owned and controlled by the people who use it, producers, consumers, or workers with similar needs who pool their resources for mutual gain is called cooperative.
Conscientiou-ness	Conscientiousness is the trait of being painstaking and careful, or the quality of being in accord with the dictates of one's conscience.Conscientiousness includes traits such as self-discipline, carefulness, thoroughness, orderedness, deliberation (the tendency to think carefully before acting) and need for achievement.
Interest	In finance and economics, interest is the price paid by a borrower for the use of a lender's money. In other words, interest is the amount of paid to "rent" money for a period of time.
Openness	Openness refers to the extent to which an economy is open, often measured by the ratio of its trade to GDP.
Personnel	A collective term for all of the employees of an organization. Personnel is also commonly used to refer to the personnel management function or the organizational unit responsible for administering personnel programs.
Externality	Externality refers to an effect of one economic agent's actions on another, such that one agent's decisions make another better or worse off by changing their utility or cost.
Evaluation	The consumer's appraisal of the product or brand on important attributes is called evaluation.
Machiavellianism	Machiavellianism refers to a personality trait. People who possess this trait behave to gain power and to control the behavior of others.
Gain	In finance, gain is a profit or an increase in value of an investment such as a stock or bond. Gain is calculated by fair market value or the proceeds from the sale of the investment minus the sum of the purchase price and all costs associated with it.

Labor	People's physical and mental talents and efforts that are used to help produce goods and services are called labor.
Job satisfaction	Job satisfaction describes how content an individual is with his or her job. It is a relatively recent term since in previous centuries the jobs available to a particular person were often predetermined by the occupation of that person's parent.
Organizational politics	Organizational politics occurs when power sources and influence tactics are used to serve personal goals or motives.
Acquisition	A company's purchase of the property and obligations of another company is an acquisition.
Competitiveness	Competitiveness usually refers to characteristics that permit a firm to compete effectively with other firms due to low cost or superior technology, perhaps internationally.
Senior executive	Senior executive means a chief executive officer, chief operating officer, chief financial officer and anyone in charge of a principal business unit or function.
Comprehensive	A comprehensive refers to a layout accurate in size, color, scheme, and other necessary details to show how a final ad will look. For presentation only, never for reproduction.
External locus of control	The belief by individuals that their future is not within their control but rather is influenced by external forces is referred to as external locus of control.
Materialism	Materialism refers to how a person or group chooses to spend their resources, particularly money and time. In common use, the word more specifically refers to a person who primarily pursues wealth and luxury. Sometimes such a person displays conspicuous consumption.
Matching	Matching refers to an accounting concept that establishes when expenses are recognized. Expenses are matched with the revenues they helped to generate and are recognized when those revenues are recognized.
Preference	The act of a debtor in paying or securing one or more of his creditors in a manner more favorable to them than to other creditors or to the exclusion of such other creditors is a preference. In the absence of statute, a preference is perfectly good, but to be legal it must be bona fide, and not a mere subterfuge of the debtor to secure a future benefit to himself or to prevent the application of his property to his debts.
Inventory	Tangible property held for sale in the normal course of business or used in producing goods or services for sale is an inventory.
Respondent	Respondent refers to a term often used to describe the party charged in an administrative proceeding. The party adverse to the appellant in a case appealed to a higher court.
Turnover	Turnover in a financial context refers to the rate at which a provider of goods cycles through its average inventory. Turnover in a human resources context refers to the characteristic of a given company or industry, relative to rate at which an employer gains and loses staff.
Prentice Hall	Prentice Hall is a leading educational publisher. It is an imprint of the Pearson Education Company, based in New Jersey, USA.
Research report	A research report is a business report produced by business research firms by their financial analysts. They are designed to dig out the important pieces of companies operational and financial reporting to paint a picture of the future of companies to assist debt and equity investing.
Points	Loan origination fees that may be deductible as interest by a buyer of property. A seller of property who pays points reduces the selling price by the amount of the points paid for the buyer.

Administrator	Administrator refers to the personal representative appointed by a probate court to settle the estate of a deceased person who died.
Manufacturing	Production of goods primarily by the application of labor and capital to raw materials and other intermediate inputs, in contrast to agriculture, mining, forestry, fishing, and services a manufacturing.
Industry	A group of firms that produce identical or similar products is an industry. It is also used specifically to refer to an area of economic production focused on manufacturing which involves large amounts of capital investment before any profit can be realized, also called "heavy industry".
Damages	The sum of money recoverable by a plaintiff who has received a judgment in a civil case is called damages.
Layoff	A layoff is the termination of an employee or (more commonly) a group of employees for business reasons, such as the decision that certain positions are no longer necessary.
Emotional labor	Emotional labor is a form of task that requires someone to suppress or simulate their emotions, particularly related to capitalistic working conditions.
Service	Service refers to a “non tangible product” that is not embodied in a physical good and that typically effects some change in another product, person, or institution. Contrasts with good.
Depression	Depression refers to a prolonged period characterized by high unemployment, low output and investment, depressed business confidence, falling prices, and widespread business failures. A milder form of business downturn is a recession.
Emotional intelligence	The ability to understand one's own emotions and the emotions of people with whom one interacts on a daily basis is referred to as the emotional intelligence.
Promotion	Promotion refers to all the techniques sellers use to motivate people to buy products or services. An attempt by marketers to inform people about products and to persuade them to participate in an exchange.
Exchange	The trade of things of value between buyer and seller so that each is better off after the trade is called the exchange.
Security	Security refers to a claim on the borrower future income that is sold by the borrower to the lender. A security is a type of transferable interest representing financial value.
Workplace behavior	The pattern of action by the members of an organization that directly or indirectly influences organizational effectiveness is workplace behavior.
Consultant	A professional that provides expert advice in a particular field or area in which customers occassionaly require this type of knowledge is a consultant.

Thomas Edison	Thomas Edison was one of the first inventors to apply the principles of mass production to the process of invention, and can therefore be credited with the creation of the first industrial research laboratory. He developed many devices which greatly influenced life in the 20th century.
Hierarchy of needs	Hierarchy of needs refers to Maslow's theory that human needs are arranged in an order or hierarchy based on their importance. The need hierarchy includes physiological, safety, social-love and belonging, esteem, and self-actualization needs.
Needs theory	Henry Murray (1893-1988), developed a personality theory during the 1930s up to the 1960s, which he called the Needs Theory. A need in this theory is defined as 'the potentiality or readiness to respond in a certain way under given circumstances'.
Hierarchy	A system of grouping people in an organization according to rank from the top down in which all subordinate managers must report to one person is called a hierarchy.
Theory X	Theory X refers to concept described by Douglas McGregor indicating an approach to management that takes a negative and pessimistic view of workers.
Theory Y	Theory Y refers to concept described by Douglas McGregor reflecting an approach to management that takes a positive and optimistic perspective on workers.
Maslow	Maslow was an American psychologist. He is mostly noted today for his proposal of a hierarchy of human needs.
Contract	A contract is a "promise" or an "agreement" that is enforced or recognized by the law. In the civil law, a contract is considered to be part of the general law of obligations.
Union	A worker association that bargains with employers over wages and working conditions is called a union.
Wage	The payment for the service of a unit of labor, per unit time. In trade theory, it is the only payment to labor, usually unskilled labor. In empirical work, wage data may exclude other compenzation, which must be added to get the total cost of employment.
Security	Security refers to a claim on the borrower future income that is sold by the borrower to the lender. A security is a type of transferable interest representing financial value.
Management	Management characterizes the process of leading and directing all or part of an organization, often a business, through the deployment and manipulation of resources. Early twentieth-century management writer Mary Parker Follett defined management as "the art of getting things done through people."
Job satisfaction	Job satisfaction describes how content an individual is with his or her job. It is a relatively recent term since in previous centuries the jobs available to a particular person were often predetermined by the occupation of that person's parent.
Respondent	Respondent refers to a term often used to describe the party charged in an administrative proceeding. The party adverse to the appellant in a case appealed to a higher court.
Credit	Credit refers to a recording as positive in the balance of payments, any transaction that gives rise to a payment into the country, such as an export, the sale of an asset, or borrowing from abroad.
Variable	A variable is something measured by a number; it is used to analyze what happens to other things when the size of that number changes.
Productivity	Productivity refers to the total output of goods and services in a given period of time divided by work hours.
Controlling	A management function that involves determining whether or not an organization is progressing

	toward its goals and objectives, and taking corrective action if it is not is called controlling.
Cooperative	A business owned and controlled by the people who use it, producers, consumers, or workers with similar needs who pool their resources for mutual gain is called cooperative.
Affiliation	A relationship with other websites in which a company can cross-promote and is credited for sales that accrue through their site is an affiliation.
Specificity	The property that a policy measure applies to one or a group of enterprises or industries, as opposed to all industries, is called specificity.
Assignment	A transfer of property or some right or interest is referred to as assignment.
Reinforcement theory	A motivation theory based on the relationship between a given behavior and its consequences is referred to as the reinforcement theory.
Law of effect	Law of effect refers to the observation that behavior which results in a pleasing outcome is likely to be repeated; behavior that results in an unpleasant outcome is not likely to be repeated.
Allocate	Allocate refers to the assignment of income for various tax purposes. A multistate corporation's nonbusiness income usually is distributed to the state where the nonbusiness assets are located; it is not apportioned with the rest of the entity's income.
Task significance	The measure of how much of a job has a substantial impact on the lives of other people, whether these people are in the immediate organization or in the world at large is task significance.
Operation	A standardized method or technique that is performed repetitively, often on different materials resulting in different finished goods is called an operation.
Motivating potential score	The extent to which the core characteristics of a job creates motivating conditions is the motivating potential score.
Predictive Index	Predictive Index is a copyrighted management tool for predicting, describing and measuring the work behavior and potential of individuals and groups at all organizational levels.
Task identity	The degree to which employees perceive how their job impacts the overall production of a product or service is task identity.
Core	A core is the set of feasible allocations in an economy that cannot be improved upon by subset of the set of the economy's consumers (a coalition). In construction, when the force in an element is within a certain center section, the core, the element will only be under compression.
Turnover	Turnover in a financial context refers to the rate at which a provider of goods cycles through its average inventory. Turnover in a human resources context refers to the characteristic of a given company or industry, relative to rate at which an employer gains and loses staff.
Information processing model	Information processing model refers to a model of advertising effects developed by William McGuire that views the receiver of a message as an information processor and problem solver. The model views the receiver as passing through a response hierarchy that includes a series of stages including message presentation, attention, comprehension, acceptance or yielding, retention, and behavior.
Job Characteristics Model	A conceptual framework for designing motivating jobs that create meaningful work experiences that satisfy employees' growth needs is referred to as the job characteristics model.

Equity theory	Equity theory, in Business seeks to describe a relationship between employees motivation and their perception of being treated fairly. The theory suggests that employees seek to ascribe values to their inputs and outputs.
Equity	Equity is the name given to the set of legal principles, in countries following the English common law tradition, which supplement strict rules of law where their application would operate harshly, so as to achieve what is sometimes referred to as "natural justice."
Graduation	Termination of a country's eligibility for GSP tariff preferences on the grounds that it has progressed sufficiently, in terms of per capita income or another measure, that it is no longer in need to special and differential treatment is graduation.
Inputs	The inputs used by a firm or an economy are the labor, raw materials, electricity and other resources it uses to produce its outputs.
Word of mouth	People influencing each other during their face-to-face converzations is called word of mouth.
Administration	Administration refers to the management and direction of the affairs of governments and institutions; a collective term for all policymaking officials of a government; the execution and implementation of public policy.
Policy	Similar to a script in that a policy can be a less than completely rational decision-making method. Involves the use of a pre-existing set of decision steps for any problem that presents itself.
Precedent	A previously decided court decision that is recognized as authority for the disposition of future decisions is a precedent.
Production	The creation of finished goods and services using the factors of production: land, labor, capital, entrepreneurship, and knowledge.
Contribution	In business organization law, the cash or property contributed to a business by its owners is referred to as contribution.
Expectancy theory	A process theory that proposes that motivation depends on individuals' expectations about their ability to perform tasks and receive desired rewards is called expectancy theory.
Comprehensive	A comprehensive refers to a layout accurate in size, color, scheme, and other necessary details to show how a final ad will look. For presentation only, never for reproduction.
Fringe benefits	The rewards other than wages that employees receive from their employers and that include pensions, medical and dental insurance, paid vacations, and sick leaves are referred to as fringe benefits.
Fringe benefit	Benefits such as sick-leave pay, vacation pay, pension plans, and health plans that represent additional compenzation to employees beyond base wages is a fringe benefit.
Trust	An arrangement in which shareholders of independent firms agree to give up their stock in exchange for trust certificates that entitle them to a share of the trust's common profits.
Uncertainty avoidance	The extent to which people prefer to be in clear and unambiguous situations is referred to as the uncertainty avoidance.
Power distance	Power distance refers to the degree to which the less powerful members of society expect there to be differences in the levels of power. A high score suggests that there is an expectation that some individuals wield larger amounts of power than others. Countries with high power distance rating are often characterized by a high rate of political violence.

Management by objectives	Management by objectives is a process of agreeing upon objectives within an organization so that management and employees buy in to the objectives and understand what they are.
Management	Management characterizes the process of leading and directing all or part of an organization, often a business, through the deployment and manipulation of resources. Early twentieth-century management writer Mary Parker Follett defined management as "the art of getting things done through people."
Tangible	Having a physical existence is referred to as the tangible. Personal property other than real estate, such as cars, boats, stocks, or other assets.
Appeal	Appeal refers to the act of asking an appellate court to overturn a decision after the trial court's final judgment has been entered.
Hierarchy	A system of grouping people in an organization according to rank from the top down in which all subordinate managers must report to one person is called a hierarchy.
Contribution	In business organization law, the cash or property contributed to a business by its owners is referred to as contribution.
Specificity	The property that a policy measure applies to one or a group of enterprises or industries, as opposed to all industries, is called specificity.
Performance feedback	The process of providing employees with information regarding their performance effectiveness is referred to as performance feedback.
Evaluation	The consumer's appraisal of the product or brand on important attributes is called evaluation.
Behavior modification	Behavior modification is a technique of altering an individual's reactions to stimuli through positive reinforcement and the extinction of maladaptive behavior.
Intervention	Intervention refers to an activity in which a government buys or sells its currency in the foreign exchange market in order to affect its currency's exchange rate.
Performance behaviors	The total set of work-related behaviors that the organization expects the individual to display are referred to as performance behaviors.
Technology	The body of knowledge and techniques that can be used to combine economic resources to produce goods and services is called technology.
Performance improvement	Performance improvement is the concept of measuring the output of a particular process or procedure then modifying the process or procedure in order to increase the output, increase efficiency, or increase the effectiveness of the process or procedure.
Reinforcement theory	A motivation theory based on the relationship between a given behavior and its consequences is referred to as the reinforcement theory.
General Electric	In 1876, Thomas Alva Edison opened a new laboratory in Menlo Park, New Jersey. Out of the laboratory was to come perhaps the most famous invention of all—a successful development of the incandescent electric lamp. By 1890, Edison had organized his various businesses into the Edison General Electric Company.
General Mills	In 2001, the General Mills purchased Pillsbury, although it was officially described as a "merger." While many of the Pillsbury-branded products are still manufactured by General Mills, some products had to be sold off to allow the merger since the new company would have held a very strong monopoly position.
Productivity	Productivity refers to the total output of goods and services in a given period of time divided by work hours.
Xerox	Xerox was founded in 1906 as "The Haloid Company" manufacturing photographic paper and

	equipment. The company came to prominence in 1959 with the introduction of the first plain paper photocopier using the process of xerography (electrophotography) developed by Chester Carlson, the Xerox 914.
Comprehensive	A comprehensive refers to a layout accurate in size, color, scheme, and other necessary details to show how a final ad will look. For presentation only, never for reproduction.
Production	The creation of finished goods and services using the factors of production: land, labor, capital, entrepreneurship, and knowledge.
Insurance	Insurance refers to a system by which individuals can reduce their exposure to risk of large losses by spreading the risks among a large number of persons.
Intranet	Intranet refers to a companywide network, closed to public access, that uses Internet-type technology. A set of communications links within one company that travel over the Internet but are closed to public access.
Economy	The income, expenditures, and resources that affect the cost of running a business and household are called an economy.
Policy	Similar to a script in that a policy can be a less than completely rational decision-making method. Involves the use of a pre-existing set of decision steps for any problem that presents itself.
Dealer	People who link buyers with sellers by buying and selling securities at stated prices are referred to as a dealer.
Participative management	Participative management or participatory management is the practice of empowering employees to participate in organizational decision making.
Empowerment	Giving employees the authority and responsibility to respond quickly to customer requests is called empowerment.
Job satisfaction	Job satisfaction describes how content an individual is with his or her job. It is a relatively recent term since in previous centuries the jobs available to a particular person were often predetermined by the occupation of that person's parent.
Variable	A variable is something measured by a number; it is used to analyze what happens to other things when the size of that number changes.
Stockholder	A stockholder is an individual or company (including a corporation) that legally owns one or more shares of stock in a joined stock company. The shareholders are the owners of a corporation. Companies listed at the stock market strive to enhance shareholder value.
Interest	In finance and economics, interest is the price paid by a borrower for the use of a lender's money. In other words, interest is the amount of paid to "rent" money for a period of time.
Labor	People's physical and mental talents and efforts that are used to help produce goods and services are called labor.
Firm	An organization that employs resources to produce a good or service for profit and owns and operates one or more plants is referred to as a firm.
Board of directors	The group of individuals elected by the stockholders of a corporation to oversee its operations is a board of directors.
Organizational performance	Organizational performance comprises the actual output or results of an organization as measured against its intended outputs (or goals and objectives).
Employee Stock Ownership Plans	Like profit sharing, Employee Stock Ownership Plans are based on the total organization's performance, but are measured in terms of stock price.

Employee stock ownership plan	Employee Stock Ownership Plan is a qualified employee-benefit plan in which employees are entitled and encouraged to invest in shares of the company's stock and often at a favorable price. The employer's contributions are tax deductible for the employer and tax deferred for the employee.
Stock	In financial terminology, stock is the capital raized by a corporation, through the issuance and sale of shares.
Trust	An arrangement in which shareholders of independent firms agree to give up their stock in exchange for trust certificates that entitle them to a share of the trust's common profits.
Allocate	Allocate refers to the assignment of income for various tax purposes. A multistate corporation's nonbusiness income usually is distributed to the state where the nonbusiness assets are located; it is not apportioned with the rest of the entity's income.
Possession	Possession refers to respecting real property, exclusive dominion and control such as owners of like property usually exercise over it. Manual control of personal property either as owner or as one having a qualified right in it.
Shares	Shares refer to an equity security, representing a shareholder's ownership of a corporation. Shares are one of a finite number of equal portions in the capital of a company, entitling the owner to a proportion of distributed, non-reinvested profits known as dividends and to a portion of the value of the company in case of liquidation.
Shareholder	A shareholder is an individual or company (including a corporation) that legally owns one or more shares of stock in a joined stock company.
Market	A market is, as defined in economics, a social arrangement that allows buyers and sellers to discover information and carry out a voluntary exchange of goods or services.
Points	Loan origination fees that may be deductible as interest by a buyer of property. A seller of property who pays points reduces the selling price by the amount of the points paid for the buyer.
Gain	In finance, gain is a profit or an increase in value of an investment such as a stock or bond. Gain is calculated by fair market value or the proceeds from the sale of the investment minus the sum of the purchase price and all costs associated with it.
Job rotation	A job enrichment strategy that involves moving employees from one job to another is a job rotation.
Job enlargement	A job enrichment strategy that involves combining a series of tasks into one challenging and interesting assignment is referred to as job enlargement.
Service	Service refers to a "non tangible product" that is not embodied in a physical good and that typically effects some change in another product, person, or institution. Contrasts with good.
Job enrichment	A motivational strategy that emphasizes motivating the worker through the job itself is called job enrichment.
Internal customer	An individuals or unit within the firm that receives services from other entities within the organization is an internal customer.
Bank One	On January 15, 2004, the Bank One announced that it was being acquired by J.P. Morgan Chase in a $58 billion merger. This merger was announced a few months after the proposed merger of Bank of America and FleetBoston banks. This awoke concerns about too much consolidation of the banking industry.
Credit	Credit refers to a recording as positive in the balance of payments, any transaction that gives rise to a payment into the country, such as an export, the sale of an asset, or

	borrowing from abroad.
Export	In economics, an export is any good or commodity, shipped or otherwise transported out of a country, province, town to another part of the world in a legitimate fashion, typically for use in trade or sale.
International trade	The export of goods and services from a country and the import of goods and services into a country is referred to as the international trade.
Export transactions	A sale of a good or service that increases the amount of foreign currency flowing to a nation's citizens, firms, and government are called export transactions.
Turnover	Turnover in a financial context refers to the rate at which a provider of goods cycles through its average inventory. Turnover in a human resources context refers to the characteristic of a given company or industry, relative to rate at which an employer gains and loses staff.
Flextime	A scheduling method that gives employees control over their work schedule is flextime; usually involves some 'core' times when employees must be at work, and a set of 'flextime' that can be adjustable for various employees.
Core time	Core time in a flextime plan, the period when all employees are expected to be at their job stations.
Core	A core is the set of feasible allocations in an economy that cannot be improved upon by subset of the set of the economy's consumers (a coalition). In construction, when the force in an element is within a certain center section, the core, the element will only be under compression.
Drawback	Drawback refers to rebate of import duties when the imported good is re-exported or used as input to the production of an exported good.
Personnel	A collective term for all of the employees of an organization. Personnel is also commonly used to refer to the personnel management function or the organizational unit responsible for administering personnel programs.
Option	A contract that gives the purchaser the option to buy or sell the underlying financial instrument at a specified price, called the exercise price or strike price, within a specific period of time.
Job sharing	Situation in which the duties and hours of one job position are carried out by two people is job sharing.
Innovation	Innovation refers to the first commercially successful introduction of a new product, the use of a new method of production, or the creation of a new form of business organization.
Verizon	Verizon a Dow 30 company, is a broadband and telecommunications provider. The acquisition of GTE by Bell Atlantic, on June 30, 2000, which formed Verizon, was among the largest mergers in United States business history. Verizon, with MCI, is currently the second largest telecommunications company in the United States.
Balance	In banking and accountancy, the outstanding balance is the amount of money owned, (or due), that remains in a deposit account (or a loan account) at a given date, after all past remittances, payments and withdrawal have been accounted for. It can be positive (then, in the balance sheet of a firm, it is an asset) or negative (a liability).
Layoff	A layoff is the termination of an employee or (more commonly) a group of employees for business reasons, such as the decision that certain positions are no longer necessary.
Telecommuting	Telecommuting is a work arrangement in which employees enjoy limited flexibility in working location and hours.

Analyst	Analyst refers to a person or tool with a primary function of information analysis, generally with a more limited, practical and short term set of goals than a researcher.
Merrill Lynch	Merrill Lynch through its subsidiaries and affiliates, provides capital markets services, investment banking and advisory services, wealth management, asset management, insurance, banking and related products and services on a global basis. It is best known for its Global Private Client services and its strong sales force.
Telecommute	To work at home and keep in touch with the company through telecommunications is referred to as telecommute.
Recruitment	Recruitment refers to the set of activities used to obtain a sufficient number of the right people at the right time; its purpose is to select those who best meet the needs of the organization.
Investment	Investment refers to spending for the production and accumulation of capital and additions to inventories. In a financial sense, buying an asset with the expectation of making a return.
Teamwork	That which occurs when group members work together in ways that utilize their skills well to accomplish a purpose is called teamwork.
Promotion	Promotion refers to all the techniques sellers use to motivate people to buy products or services. An attempt by marketers to inform people about products and to persuade them to participate in an exchange.
Expectancy theory	A process theory that proposes that motivation depends on individuals' expectations about their ability to perform tasks and receive desired rewards is called expectancy theory.
Flexible work schedule	A flexible work schedule is a shedule in which an employee has a forty hour work week but can set their own schedule within the limits set by the employer.
Manufacturing	Production of goods primarily by the application of labor and capital to raw materials and other intermediate inputs, in contrast to agriculture, mining, forestry, fishing, and services a manufacturing.
Recession	A significant decline in economic activity. In the U.S., recession is approximately defined as two successive quarters of falling GDP, as judged by NBER.
American Express	From the early 1980s until the late 1990s, American Express was known for cutting its merchant fees (also known as a "discount rate") to fine merchants and restaurants if they only accepted American Express and no other credit or charge cards. This prompted competitors such as Visa and MasterCard to cry foul for a while, as the tactics "locked" restaurants into American Express.
Profit sharing	A compenzation plan in which payments are based on a measure of organization performance and do not become part of the employees' base salary is profit sharing.
Gainsharing	A form of group compenzation based on group or plant performance that does not become part of the employee's base salary is gainsharing.
Incentive	An incentive is any factor (financial or non-financial) that provides a motive for a particular course of action, or counts as a reason for preferring one choice to the alternatives.
Profit	Profit refers to the return to the resource entrepreneurial ability; total revenue minus total cost.
Wage	The payment for the service of a unit of labor, per unit time. In trade theory, it is the only payment to labor, usually unskilled labor. In empirical work, wage data may exclude other compenzation, which must be added to get the total cost of employment.

Annuity	A contract to make regular payments to a person for life or for a fixed period is an annuity.
Variable cost	The portion of a firm or industry's cost that changes with output, in contrast to fixed cost is referred to as variable cost.
Expense	In accounting, an expense represents an event in which an asset is used up or a liability is incurred. In terms of the accounting equation, expenses reduce owners' equity.
Stock option	A stock option is a specific type of option that uses the stock itself as an underlying instrument to determine the option's pay-off and therefore its value.
Gainsharing plan	An incentive system that specified a formula by which the cost savings from productivity gains achieved by a company are shared with the workers who helped accomplish the improvements is called a gainsharing plan.
American Management Association	American Management Association International is the world's largest membership-based management development and executive training organization. Their products include instructor led seminars, workshops, conferences, customized corporate programs, online learning, books, newsletters, research surveys and reports.
Grievance	A charge by employees that management is not abiding by the terms of the negotiated labormanagement agreement is the grievance.
Extension	Extension refers to an out-of-court settlement in which creditors agree to allow the firm more time to meet its financial obligations. A new repayment schedule will be developed, subject to the acceptance of creditors.
Fixed expense	A fixed expense is an expense that remains constant as activity changes within the relevant range. Any costs not related directly to the production of your product or service.
Trend	Trend refers to the long-term movement of an economic variable, such as its average rate of increase or decrease over enough years to encompass several business cycles.
Firestone Tire	The Firestone Tire and Rubber Company was founded to supply pneumatic tires for wagons, buggies, and other forms of wheeled transportation common in the era. They soon saw the huge potential for marketing tires for automobiles and befriended Henry Ford, the first industrialist to produce them using the techniques of mass production. This relationship was used to become the original equipment supplier of Ford Motor Company automobiles, and was also active in the replacement market.
Staffing	Staffing refers to a management function that includes hiring, motivating, and retaining the best people available to accomplish the company's objectives.
Downsizing	The process of eliminating managerial and non-managerial positions are called downsizing.
Specialist	A specialist is a trader who makes a market in one or several stocks and holds the limit order book for those stocks.
Assessment	Collecting information and providing feedback to employees about their behavior, communication style, or skills is an assessment.
Hierarchy of needs	Hierarchy of needs refers to Maslow's theory that human needs are arranged in an order or hierarchy based on their importance. The need hierarchy includes physiological, safety, social-love and belonging, esteem, and self-actualization needs.
Needs theory	Henry Murray (1893-1988), developed a personality theory during the 1930s up to the 1960s, which he called the Needs Theory. A need in this theory is defined as 'the potentiality or readiness to respond in a certain way under given circumstances'.
Maslow	Maslow was an American psychologist. He is mostly noted today for his proposal of a hierarchy of human needs.

Equity	Equity is the name given to the set of legal principles, in countries following the English common law tradition, which supplement strict rules of law where their application would operate harshly, so as to achieve what is sometimes referred to as "natural justice."
Market value	Market value refers to the price of an asset agreed on between a willing buyer and a willing seller; the price an asset could demand if it is sold on the open market.

Manufacturing	Production of goods primarily by the application of labor and capital to raw materials and other intermediate inputs, in contrast to agriculture, mining, forestry, fishing, and services a manufacturing.
Service	Service refers to a "non tangible product" that is not embodied in a physical good and that typically effects some change in another product, person, or institution. Contrasts with good.
Production	The creation of finished goods and services using the factors of production: land, labor, capital, entrepreneurship, and knowledge.
Expense	In accounting, an expense represents an event in which an asset is used up or a liability is incurred. In terms of the accounting equation, expenses reduce owners' equity.
Complete information	Complete information refers to the assumption that economic agents know everything that they need to know in order to make optimal decisions. Types of incomplete information are uncertainty and asymmetric information.
Yield	The interest rate that equates a future value or an annuity to a given present value is a yield.
Foundation	A Foundation is a type of philanthropic organization set up by either individuals or institutions as a legal entity (either as a corporation or trust) with the purpose of distributing grants to support causes in line with the goals of the foundation.
Contribution	In business organization law, the cash or property contributed to a business by its owners is referred to as contribution.
Analogy	Analogy is either the cognitive process of transferring information from a particular subject to another particular subject (the target), or a linguistic expression corresponding to such a process. In a narrower sense, analogy is an inference or an argument from a particular to another particular, as opposed to deduction, induction, and abduction, where at least one of the premises or the conclusion is general.
Bounded rationality	The understanding that rational decisions are very much bounded or constrained by practical constraints is referred to as bounded rationality.
Evaluation	The consumer's appraisal of the product or brand on important attributes is called evaluation.
Satisficing	Satisficing refers to a method for making decisions under bounded rationality; to choose the first option that meets a set of minimal criteria that have been established.
Status quo	Status quo is a Latin term meaning the present, current, existing state of affairs.
Creep	Creep is a problem in project management where the initial objectives of the project are jeopardized by a gradual increase in overall objectives as the project progresses.
Overconfidence bias	The overconfidence bias refers to the human tendency to be more confident in one's estimates or forecasts of a firm than one ought to be.
Advertising	Advertising refers to paid, nonpersonal communication through various media by organizations and individuals who are in some way identified in the advertising message.
Management	Management characterizes the process of leading and directing all or part of an organization, often a business, through the deployment and manipulation of resources. Early twentieth-century management writer Mary Parker Follett defined management as "the art of getting things done through people."
Estate	An estate is the totality of the legal rights, interests, entitlements and obligations attaching to property. In the context of wills and probate, it refers to the totality of the

	property which the deceased owned or in which some interest was held.
Negotiation	Negotiation is the process whereby interested parties resolve disputes, agree upon courses of action, bargain for individual or collective advantage, and/or attempt to craft outcomes which serve their mutual interests.
Assessment	Collecting information and providing feedback to employees about their behavior, communication style, or skills is an assessment.
Applicant	In many tribunal and administrative law suits, the person who initiates the claim is called the applicant.
Availability bias	Availability bias is the tendency to judge probability by how easily examples can be brought to mind.
Performance appraisal	An evaluation in which the performance level of employees is measured against established standards to make decisions about promotions, compenzation, additional training, or firing is referred to as performance appraisal.
Escalation of commitment	Escalation of commitment is the phenomenon where people increase their investment in a decision despite new evidence suggesting that the decision was probably wrong.
Escalation	Regarding the structure of tariffs. In the context of a trade war, escalation refers to the increase in tariffs that occurs as countries retaliate again and again.
Distortion	Distortion refers to any departure from the ideal of perfect competition that interferes with economic agents maximizing social welfare when they maximize their own.
Effective manager	Leader of a team that consistently achieves high performance goals is an effective manager.
Stock	In financial terminology, stock is the capital raized by a corporation, through the issuance and sale of shares.
Hindsight bias	Hindsight bias, sometimes called the I-knew-it-all-along effect, is the inclination to see past events as being predictable and reasonable to expect, perhaps because they are more available than possible outcomes which did not occur.
Complement	A good that is used in conjunction with another good is a complement. For example, cameras and film would complement eachother.
Precedent	A previously decided court decision that is recognized as authority for the disposition of future decisions is a precedent.
Argument	The discussion by counsel for the respective parties of their contentions on the law and the facts of the case being tried in order to aid the jury in arriving at a correct and just conclusion is called argument.
Variable	A variable is something measured by a number; it is used to analyze what happens to other things when the size of that number changes.
Option	A contract that gives the purchaser the option to buy or sell the underlying financial instrument at a specified price, called the exercise price or strike price, within a specific period of time.
Short run	Short run refers to a period of time that permits an increase or decrease in current production volume with existing capacity, but one that is too short to permit enlargement of that capacity itself (eg, the building of new plants, training of additional workers, etc.).
Behavioral style	Behavioral style refers to decision making that is very attuned to how decisions affect employees and the work environment; tends to be more deliberate and slower in style.

Analytic style	Analytic style refers to a style characteristic of someone who approaches decisions in a highly rational way and who is capable of tolerating uncertainty/ambiguity.
Consideration	Consideration in contract law, a basic requirement for an enforceable agreement under traditional contract principles, defined in this text as legal value, bargained for and given in exchange for an act or promise. In corporation law, cash or property contributed to a corporation in exchange for shares, or a promise to contribute such cash or property.
Depression	Depression refers to a prolonged period characterized by high unemployment, low output and investment, depressed business confidence, falling prices, and widespread business failures. A milder form of business downturn is a recession.
Exchange	The trade of things of value between buyer and seller so that each is better off after the trade is called the exchange.
Authority	Authority in agency law, refers to an agent's ability to affect his principal's legal relations with third parties. Also used to refer to an actor's legal power or ability to do something. In addition, sometimes used to refer to a statute, case, or other legal source that justifies a particular result.
Regulation	Regulation refers to restrictions state and federal laws place on business with regard to the conduct of its activities.
General Motors	General Motors is the world's largest automaker. Founded in 1908, today it employs about 327,000 people around the world. With global headquarters in Detroit, it manufactures its cars and trucks in 33 countries.
Promotion	Promotion refers to all the techniques sellers use to motivate people to buy products or services. An attempt by marketers to inform people about products and to persuade them to participate in an exchange.
New product development	New product development is the complete process of bringing a new product to market. There are two parallel aspects to this process : one involves product engineering ; the other marketing analysis.
Committee	A long-lasting, sometimes permanent team in the organization structure created to deal with tasks that recur regularly is the committee.
Product development	In business and engineering, new product development is the complete process of bringing a new product to market. There are two parallel aspects to this process : one involves product engineering ; the other marketing analysis. Marketers see new product development as the first stage in product life cycle management, engineers as part of Product Lifecycle Management.
Budget	Budget refers to an account, usually for a year, of the planned expenditures and the expected receipts of an entity. For a government, the receipts are tax revenues.
Time orientation	The extent to which members of a culture adopt a long term versus a short term outlook on work is time orientation.
Utilitarianism	The political philosophy according to which the government should choose policies to maximize the total utility of everyone in society is called utilitarianism.
Productivity	Productivity refers to the total output of goods and services in a given period of time divided by work hours.
Profit	Profit refers to the return to the resource entrepreneurial ability; total revenue minus total cost.
Due process	Due process of law is a legal concept that ensures the government will respect all of a person's legal rights instead of just some or most of those legal rights when the government

deprives a person of life, liberty, or property.

Layoff | A layoff is the termination of an employee or (more commonly) a group of employees for business reasons, such as the decision that certain positions are no longer necessary.

Wage | The payment for the service of a unit of labor, per unit time. In trade theory, it is the only payment to labor, usually unskilled labor. In empirical work, wage data may exclude other compenzation, which must be added to get the total cost of employment.

Innovation | Innovation refers to the first commercially successful introduction of a new product, the use of a new method of production, or the creation of a new form of business organization.

Interest | In finance and economics, interest is the price paid by a borrower for the use of a lender's money. In other words, interest is the amount of paid to "rent" money for a period of time.

Stockholder | A stockholder is an individual or company (including a corporation) that legally owns one or more shares of stock in a joined stock company. The shareholders are the owners of a corporation. Companies listed at the stock market strive to enhance shareholder value.

Closing | The finalization of a real estate sales transaction that passes title to the property from the seller to the buyer is referred to as a closing. Closing is a sales term which refers to the process of making a sale. It refers to reaching the final step, which may be an exchange of money or acquiring a signature.

Gain | In finance, gain is a profit or an increase in value of an investment such as a stock or bond. Gain is calculated by fair market value or the proceeds from the sale of the investment minus the sum of the purchase price and all costs associated with it.

Analyst | Analyst refers to a person or tool with a primary function of information analysis, generally with a more limited, practical and short term set of goals than a researcher.

Market | A market is, as defined in economics, a social arrangement that allows buyers and sellers to discover information and carry out a voluntary exchange of goods or services.

Assignment	A transfer of property or some right or interest is referred to as assignment.
Organizational goals	Objectives that management seeks to achieve in pursuing the firm's purpose are organizational goals.
Interest	In finance and economics, interest is the price paid by a borrower for the use of a lender's money. In other words, interest is the amount of paid to "rent" money for a period of time.
Task group	Task group refers to a relatively temporary, formal group established to do a specific task.
Formal organization	Formal organization refers to the structure that details lines of responsibility, authority, and position; that is, the structure shown on organization charts.
Command group	Command group refers to a relatively permanent, formal group with functional reporting relationships; usually included in the organization chart.
Principal	In agency law, one under whose direction an agent acts and for whose benefit that agent acts is a principal.
Audit	An examination of the financial reports to ensure that they represent what they claim and conform with generally accepted accounting principles is referred to as audit.
Fringe benefits	The rewards other than wages that employees receive from their employers and that include pensions, medical and dental insurance, paid vacations, and sick leaves are referred to as fringe benefits.
Fringe benefit	Benefits such as sick-leave pay, vacation pay, pension plans, and health plans that represent additional compenzation to employees beyond base wages is a fringe benefit.
Holding	The holding is a court's determination of a matter of law based on the issue presented in the particular case. In other words: under this law, with these facts, this result.
Standing	Standing refers to the legal requirement that anyone seeking to challenge a particular action in court must demonstrate that such action substantially affects his legitimate interests before he will be entitled to bring suit.
Management	Management characterizes the process of leading and directing all or part of an organization, often a business, through the deployment and manipulation of resources. Early twentieth-century management writer Mary Parker Follett defined management as "the art of getting things done through people."
Buyer	A buyer refers to a role in the buying center with formal authority and responsibility to select the supplier and negotiate the terms of the contract.
Labor	People's physical and mental talents and efforts that are used to help produce goods and services are called labor.
Task force	A temporary team or committee formed to solve a specific short-term problem involving several departments is the task force.
Psychological contract	A person's set of expectations regarding what he or she will contribute to the organization and what the organization, in return, will provide to the individual is called psychological contract.
Contract	A contract is a "promise" or an "agreement" that is enforced or recognized by the law. In the civil law, a contract is considered to be part of the general law of obligations.
Loyalty	Marketers tend to define customer loyalty as making repeat purchases. Some argue that it should be defined attitudinally as a strongly positive feeling about the brand.
Role conflict	Role conflict is a special form of social conflict that takes place when one is forced to take on two different and incompatible roles at the same time.

Compliance	A type of influence process where a receiver accepts the position advocated by a source to obtain favorable outcomes or to avoid punishment is the compliance.
Channel	Channel, in communications (sometimes called communications channel), refers to the medium used to convey information from a sender (or transmitter) to a receiver.
Communication channel	The pathways through which messages are communicated are called a communication channel.
Appreciation	Appreciation refers to a rise in the value of a country's currency on the exchange market, relative either to a particular other currency or to a weighted average of other currencies. The currency is said to appreciate. Opposite of 'depreciation.' Appreciation can also refer to the increase in value of any asset.
Productivity	Productivity refers to the total output of goods and services in a given period of time divided by work hours.
Production	The creation of finished goods and services using the factors of production: land, labor, capital, entrepreneurship, and knowledge.
Incentive	An incentive is any factor (financial or non-financial) that provides a motive for a particular course of action, or counts as a reason for preferring one choice to the alternatives.
Wage	The payment for the service of a unit of labor, per unit time. In trade theory, it is the only payment to labor, usually unskilled labor. In empirical work, wage data may exclude other compenzation, which must be added to get the total cost of employment.
Layoff	A layoff is the termination of an employee or (more commonly) a group of employees for business reasons, such as the decision that certain positions are no longer necessary.
Contribution	In business organization law, the cash or property contributed to a business by its owners is referred to as contribution.
Matching	Matching refers to an accounting concept that establishes when expenses are recognized. Expenses are matched with the revenues they helped to generate and are recognized when those revenues are recognized.
Trial	An examination before a competent tribunal, according to the law of the land, of the facts or law put in issue in a cause, for the purpose of determining such issue is a trial. When the court hears and determines any issue of fact or law for the purpose of determining the rights of the parties, it may be considered a trial.
Disparity	Disparity refers to the regional and economic differences in a country, province, state, or continent
Aid	Assistance provided by countries and by international institutions such as the World Bank to developing countries in the form of monetary grants, loans at low interest rates, in kind, or a combination of these is called aid. Aid can also refer to assistance of any type rendered to benefit some group or individual.
Hierarchy	A system of grouping people in an organization according to rank from the top down in which all subordinate managers must report to one person is called a hierarchy.
Equity	Equity is the name given to the set of legal principles, in countries following the English common law tradition, which supplement strict rules of law where their application would operate harshly, so as to achieve what is sometimes referred to as "natural justice."
Disequilibrium	Inequality or imbalance of supply and demand is referred to as disequilibrium.
Preparation	Preparation refers to usually the first stage in the creative process. It includes education

and formal training.

Promotion Promotion refers to all the techniques sellers use to motivate people to buy products or services. An attempt by marketers to inform people about products and to persuade them to participate in an exchange.

Insurance Insurance refers to a system by which individuals can reduce their exposure to risk of large losses by spreading the risks among a large number of persons.

Industry A group of firms that produce identical or similar products is an industry. It is also used specifically to refer to an area of economic production focused on manufacturing which involves large amounts of capital investment before any profit can be realized, also called "heavy industry".

Agent A person who makes economic decisions for another economic actor. A hired manager operates as an agent for a firm's owner.

Budget Budget refers to an account, usually for a year, of the planned expenditures and the expected receipts of an entity. For a government, the receipts are tax revenues.

Social class Social class refers to the hierarchical distinctions between individuals or groups in societies or cultures. While anthropologists, historians and sociologists identify class as a social structure emerging from pre-history, the idea of social class entered the English lexicon about the 1770s.

Social loafing Social loafing is a tendency for a team member to put out less effort than they would if they were working alone. Freeloading such as this can occur when members' performance melds in and they can hide in the crowd.

Free rider Free rider refers to someone who enjoys the benefits of a public good without bearing the cost. An example, in trade policy, is that trade liberalization benefits the majority of consumers without their lobbying for it.

Composition An out-of-court settlement in which creditors agree to accept a fractional settlement on their original claim is referred to as composition.

Homogeneous In the context of procurement/purchasing, homogeneous is used to describe goods that do not vary in their essential characteristic irrespective of the source of supply.

Asset An item of property, such as land, capital, money, a share in ownership, or a claim on others for future payment, such as a bond or a bank deposit is an asset.

Demographic A demographic is a term used in marketing and broadcasting, to describe a demographic grouping or a market segment.

Turnover Turnover in a financial context refers to the rate at which a provider of goods cycles through its average inventory. Turnover in a human resources context refers to the characteristic of a given company or industry, relative to rate at which an employer gains and loses staff.

Service Service refers to a “non tangible product” that is not embodied in a physical good and that typically effects some change in another product, person, or institution. Contrasts with good.

Great Depression The period of severe economic contraction and high unemployment that began in 1929 and continued throughout the 1930s is referred to as the Great Depression.

Depression Depression refers to a prolonged period characterized by high unemployment, low output and investment, depressed business confidence, falling prices, and widespread business failures. A milder form of business downturn is a recession.

Legal system	Legal system refers to system of rules that regulate behavior and the processes by which the laws of a country are enforced and through which redress of grievances is obtained.
Jury	A body of lay persons, selected by lot, or by some other fair and impartial means, to ascertain, under the guidance of the judge, the truth in questions of fact arising either in civil litigation or a criminal process is referred to as jury.
Complete information	Complete information refers to the assumption that economic agents know everything that they need to know in order to make optimal decisions. Types of incomplete information are uncertainty and asymmetric information.
Groupthink	Groupthink is a situation in which pressures for cohesion and togetherness are so strong as to produce narrowly considered and bad decisions; this can be especially true via conformity pressures in groups.
Byproduct	A byproduct is a secondary or incidental product deriving from a manufacturing process or chemical reaction, and is not the primary product or service being produced.
Variable	A variable is something measured by a number; it is used to analyze what happens to other things when the size of that number changes.
Nominal group technique	Nominal group technique refers to a more elaborate attempt to separate the generation from the evaluation of ideas in group settings. With the nominal group method, ideas are generated in private and circulated among the group later.
Nominal group	A nominal category or a nominal group is a group of objects or ideas that can be collectively grouped on the basis of shared, arbitrary characteristic.
Brainstorming	Brainstorming refers to a technique designed to overcome our natural tendency to evaluate and criticize ideas and thereby reduce the creative output of those ideas. People are encouraged to produce ideas/options without criticizing, often at a very fast pace to minimize our natural tendency to criticize.
Committee	A long-lasting, sometimes permanent team in the organization structure created to deal with tasks that recur regularly is the committee.
Technology	The body of knowledge and techniques that can be used to combine economic resources to produce goods and services is called technology.
Evaluation	The consumer's appraisal of the product or brand on important attributes is called evaluation.
Alignment	Term that refers to optimal coordination among disparate departments and divisions within a firm is referred to as alignment.
Teamwork	That which occurs when group members work together in ways that utilize their skills well to accomplish a purpose is called teamwork.
Gain	In finance, gain is a profit or an increase in value of an investment such as a stock or bond. Gain is calculated by fair market value or the proceeds from the sale of the investment minus the sum of the purchase price and all costs associated with it.

Management	Management characterizes the process of leading and directing all or part of an organization, often a business, through the deployment and manipulation of resources. Early twentieth-century management writer Mary Parker Follett defined management as "the art of getting things done through people."
Operation	A standardized method or technique that is performed repetitively, often on different materials resulting in different finished goods is called an operation.
Trend	Trend refers to the long-term movement of an economic variable, such as its average rate of increase or decrease over enough years to encompass several business cycles.
Firm	An organization that employs resources to produce a good or service for profit and owns and operates one or more plants is referred to as a firm.
Production	The creation of finished goods and services using the factors of production: land, labor, capital, entrepreneurship, and knowledge.
General Electric	In 1876, Thomas Alva Edison opened a new laboratory in Menlo Park, New Jersey. Out of the laboratory was to come perhaps the most famous invention of all—a successful development of the incandescent electric lamp. By 1890, Edison had organized his various businesses into the Edison General Electric Company.
DaimlerChrysler	In 2002, the merged company, DaimlerChrysler, appeared to run two independent product lines, with few signs of corporate integration. In 2003, however, it was alleged by the Detroit News that the "merger of equals" was, in fact, a takeover.
Apple Computer	Apple Computer has been a major player in the evolution of personal computing since its founding in 1976. The Apple II microcomputer, introduced in 1977, was a hit with home users.
John Deere	John Deere (February 7, 1804 - May 17, 1886) was an American blacksmith and manufacturer who founded one of the largest agricultural and construction equipment manufacturers in the world.
Insurance	Insurance refers to a system by which individuals can reduce their exposure to risk of large losses by spreading the risks among a large number of persons.
Motorola	The Six Sigma quality system was developed at Motorola even though it became most well known because of its use by General Electric. It was created by engineer Bill Smith, under the direction of Bob Galvin (son of founder Paul Galvin) when he was running the company.
Boeing	Boeing is the world's largest aircraft manufacturer by revenue. Headquartered in Chicago, Illinois, Boeing is the second-largest defense contractor in the world. In 2005, the company was the world's largest civil aircraft manufacturer in terms of value.
Synergy	Corporate synergy occurs when corporations interact congruently. A corporate synergy refers to a financial benefit that a corporation expects to realize when it merges with or acquires another corporation.
Inputs	The inputs used by a firm or an economy are the labor, raw materials, electricity and other resources it uses to produce its outputs.
Organizational performance	Organizational performance comprises the actual output or results of an organization as measured against its intended outputs (or goals and objectives).
Gain	In finance, gain is a profit or an increase in value of an investment such as a stock or bond. Gain is calculated by fair market value or the proceeds from the sale of the investment minus the sum of the purchase price and all costs associated with it.
Authority	Authority in agency law, refers to an agent's ability to affect his principal's legal relations with third parties. Also used to refer to an actor's legal power or ability to do something. In addition, sometimes used to refer to a statute, case, or other legal source

	that justifies a particular result.
Quality circle	A quality circle is a volunteer group composed of workers who meet together to discuss workplace improvement, and make presentations to management with their ideas.
Supervisor	A Supervisor is an employee of an organization with some of the powers and responsibilities of management, occupying a role between true manager and a regular employee. A Supervisor position is typically the first step towards being promoted into a management role.
Assembly line	An assembly line is a manufacturing process in which interchangeable parts are added to a product in a sequential manner to create a finished product.
Productivity	Productivity refers to the total output of goods and services in a given period of time divided by work hours.
Manufacturing	Production of goods primarily by the application of labor and capital to raw materials and other intermediate inputs, in contrast to agriculture, mining, forestry, fishing, and services a manufacturing.
Job satisfaction	Job satisfaction describes how content an individual is with his or her job. It is a relatively recent term since in previous centuries the jobs available to a particular person were often predetermined by the occupation of that person's parent.
Turnover	Turnover in a financial context refers to the rate at which a provider of goods cycles through its average inventory. Turnover in a human resources context refers to the characteristic of a given company or industry, relative to rate at which an employer gains and loses staff.
Downsizing	The process of eliminating managerial and non-managerial positions are called downsizing.
Teamwork	That which occurs when group members work together in ways that utilize their skills well to accomplish a purpose is called teamwork.
Trust	An arrangement in which shareholders of independent firms agree to give up their stock in exchange for trust certificates that entitle them to a share of the trust's common profits.
Virtual team	A group of physically dispersed people who work as a team via alternative communication modes is called virtual team.
Technology	The body of knowledge and techniques that can be used to combine economic resources to produce goods and services is called technology.
Body language	Body language is a broad term for forms of communication using body movements or gestures instead of, or in addition to, sounds, verbal language, or other forms of communication.
Exchange	The trade of things of value between buyer and seller so that each is better off after the trade is called the exchange.
Users	Users refer to people in the organization who actually use the product or service purchased by the buying center.
Ford	Ford is an American company that manufactures and sells automobiles worldwide. Ford introduced methods for large-scale manufacturing of cars, and large-scale management of an industrial workforce, especially elaborately engineered manufacturing sequences typified by the moving assembly lines.
Credit	Credit refers to a recording as positive in the balance of payments, any transaction that gives rise to a payment into the country, such as an export, the sale of an asset, or borrowing from abroad.
Task significance	The measure of how much of a job has a substantial impact on the lives of other people, whether these people are in the immediate organization or in the world at large is task

significance.

Social loafing Social loafing is a tendency for a team member to put out less effort than they would if they were working alone. Freeloading such as this can occur when members' performance melds in and they can hide in the crowd.

Task identity The degree to which employees perceive how their job impacts the overall production of a product or service is task identity.

Composition An out-of-court settlement in which creditors agree to accept a fractional settlement on their original claim is referred to as composition.

Preference The act of a debtor in paying or securing one or more of his creditors in a manner more favorable to them than to other creditors or to the exclusion of such other creditors is a preference. In the absence of statute, a preference is perfectly good, but to be legal it must be bona fide, and not a mere subterfuge of the debtor to secure a future benefit to himself or to prevent the application of his property to his debts.

Contribution In business organization law, the cash or property contributed to a business by its owners is referred to as contribution.

Evaluation The consumer's appraisal of the product or brand on important attributes is called evaluation.

Leadership Management merely consists of leadership applied to business situations; or in other words: management forms a sub-set of the broader process of leadership.

Context The effect of the background under which a message often takes on more and richer meaning is a context. Context is especially important in cross-cultural interactions because some cultures are said to be high context or low context.

Budget Budget refers to an account, usually for a year, of the planned expenditures and the expected receipts of an entity. For a government, the receipts are tax revenues.

Policy Similar to a script in that a policy can be a less than completely rational decision-making method. Involves the use of a pre-existing set of decision steps for any problem that presents itself.

Bond Bond refers to a debt instrument, issued by a borrower and promising a specified stream of payments to the purchaser, usually regular interest payments plus a final repayment of principal.

Incentive An incentive is any factor (financial or non-financial) that provides a motive for a particular course of action, or counts as a reason for preferring one choice to the alternatives.

Wage The payment for the service of a unit of labor, per unit time. In trade theory, it is the only payment to labor, usually unskilled labor. In empirical work, wage data may exclude other compenzation, which must be added to get the total cost of employment.

Variable A variable is something measured by a number; it is used to analyze what happens to other things when the size of that number changes.

Expense In accounting, an expense represents an event in which an asset is used up or a liability is incurred. In terms of the accounting equation, expenses reduce owners' equity.

Conscientiou-ness Conscientiousness is the trait of being painstaking and careful, or the quality of being in accord with the dictates of one's conscience.Conscientiousness includes traits such as self-discipline, carefulness, thoroughness, orderedness, deliberation (the tendency to think carefully before acting) and need for achievement.

Variance	Variance refers to a measure of how much an economic or statistical variable varies across values or observations. Its calculation is the same as that of the covariance, being the covariance of the variable with itself.
Management system	A management system is the framework of processes and procedures used to ensure that an organization can fulfill all tasks required to achieve its objectives.
Team management	Team management teaches a number of techniques that aim at forming and managing teams.
Controlling	A management function that involves determining whether or not an organization is progressing toward its goals and objectives, and taking corrective action if it is not is called controlling.
Controller	Controller refers to the financial executive primarily responsible for management accounting and financial accounting. Also called chief accounting officer.
Assessor	An assessor is an expert who calculates the value of property. The value calculated by the assessor is then used as the basis for determining the amounts to be paid or assessed for tax or insurance purposes.
Assignment	A transfer of property or some right or interest is referred to as assignment.
Allocate	Allocate refers to the assignment of income for various tax purposes. A multistate corporation's nonbusiness income usually is distributed to the state where the nonbusiness assets are located; it is not apportioned with the rest of the entity's income.
Matching	Matching refers to an accounting concept that establishes when expenses are recognized. Expenses are matched with the revenues they helped to generate and are recognized when those revenues are recognized.
Option	A contract that gives the purchaser the option to buy or sell the underlying financial instrument at a specified price, called the exercise price or strike price, within a specific period of time.
Collective responsibility	Cabinet collective responsibility is constitutional convention in the states that use the Westminster System. It means that members of the Cabinet must publicly support all governmental decisions made in Cabinet, even if they do not privately agree with them.
Assessment	Collecting information and providing feedback to employees about their behavior, communication style, or skills is an assessment.
Holding	The holding is a court's determination of a matter of law based on the issue presented in the particular case. In other words: under this law, with these facts, this result.
Collectivism	Collectivism is a term used to describe that things should be owned by the group and used for the benefit of all rather than being owned by individuals.
Points	Loan origination fees that may be deductible as interest by a buyer of property. A seller of property who pays points reduces the selling price by the amount of the points paid for the buyer.
General Motors	General Motors is the world's largest automaker. Founded in 1908, today it employs about 327,000 people around the world. With global headquarters in Detroit, it manufactures its cars and trucks in 33 countries.
Inception	The date and time on which coverage under an insurance policy takes effect is inception. Also refers to the date at which a stock or mutual fund was first traded.
Interpersonal skills	Interpersonal skills are used to communicate with, understand, and motivate individuals and groups.
Specialist	A specialist is a trader who makes a market in one or several stocks and holds the limit

	order book for those stocks.
Consultant	A professional that provides expert advice in a particular field or area in which customers occassionaly require this type of knowledge is a consultant.
Cooperative	A business owned and controlled by the people who use it, producers, consumers, or workers with similar needs who pool their resources for mutual gain is called cooperative.
Promotion	Promotion refers to all the techniques sellers use to motivate people to buy products or services. An attempt by marketers to inform people about products and to persuade them to participate in an exchange.
Intrinsic reward	Motivating events which occur as a natural part of the learning experience is a intrinsic reward.
Inventory	Tangible property held for sale in the normal course of business or used in producing goods or services for sale is an inventory.
Inventory management	The planning, coordinating, and controlling activities related to the flow of inventory into, through, and out of an organization is referred to as inventory management.
Process improvement	Process improvement is the activity of elevating the performance of a process, especially that of a business process with regard to its goal.
Control charts	Control charts refer to tools for monitoring process variation.
Control chart	The control chart, also known as the 'Shewhart chart' or 'process-behavior chart' is a statistical tool intended to assess the nature of variation in a process and to facilitate forecasting and management. The control chart is one of the seven basic tools of quality control, which include the histogram, Pareto chart, check sheet, control chart, cause-and-effect diagram, flowchart, and scatter diagram.
Task force	A temporary team or committee formed to solve a specific short-term problem involving several departments is the task force.
Horizontal communication	The lateral or diagonal exchange of messages among peers or coworkers is referred to as horizontal communication.
Service	Service refers to a "non tangible product" that is not embodied in a physical good and that typically effects some change in another product, person, or institution. Contrasts with good.
Complexity	The technical sophistication of the product and hence the amount of understanding required to use it is referred to as complexity. It is the opposite of simplicity.
Interdependence	The extent to which departments depend on each other for resources or materials to accomplish their tasks is referred to as interdependence.
Interest	In finance and economics, interest is the price paid by a borrower for the use of a lender's money. In other words, interest is the amount of paid to "rent" money for a period of time.
Conversion	Conversion refers to any distinct act of dominion wrongfully exerted over another's personal property in denial of or inconsistent with his rights therein. That tort committed by a person who deals with chattels not belonging to him in a manner that is inconsistent with the ownership of the lawful owner.

Receiver	A person that is appointed as a custodian of other people's property by a court of law or a creditor of the owner, pending a lawsuit or reorganization is called a receiver.
Hierarchy	A system of grouping people in an organization according to rank from the top down in which all subordinate managers must report to one person is called a hierarchy.
Authority	Authority in agency law, refers to an agent's ability to affect his principal's legal relations with third parties. Also used to refer to an actor's legal power or ability to do something. In addition, sometimes used to refer to a statute, case, or other legal source that justifies a particular result.
Controlling	A management function that involves determining whether or not an organization is progressing toward its goals and objectives, and taking corrective action if it is not is called controlling.
Channel	Channel, in communications (sometimes called communications channel), refers to the medium used to convey information from a sender (or transmitter) to a receiver.
Feedback loop	Feedback loop consists of a response and feedback. It is a system where outputs are fed back into the system as inputs, increasing or decreasing effects.
Downward communication	Downward communication refers to communication flows from a company or boss down to the affected employees.
Policy	Similar to a script in that a policy can be a less than completely rational decision-making method. Involves the use of a pre-existing set of decision steps for any problem that presents itself.
Management	Management characterizes the process of leading and directing all or part of an organization, often a business, through the deployment and manipulation of resources. Early twentieth-century management writer Mary Parker Follett defined management as "the art of getting things done through people."
Upward communication	A communication channel that allows for relatively free movement of messages from those lower in the organization to those at higher levels is an upward communication.
Personnel	A collective term for all of the employees of an organization. Personnel is also commonly used to refer to the personnel management function or the organizational unit responsible for administering personnel programs.
Lateral communication	Communication that flows relatively freely between people of relatively equal power in organizations is referred to as lateral communication.
Horizontal communication	The lateral or diagonal exchange of messages among peers or coworkers is referred to as horizontal communication.
Nonverbal communication	The many additional ways that communication is accomplished beyond the oral or written word is referred to as nonverbal communication.
Distortion	Distortion refers to any departure from the ideal of perfect competition that interferes with economic agents maximizing social welfare when they maximize their own.
Electronic mail	Electronic mail refers to electronic written communication between individuals using computers connected to the Internet.
Marketing Plan	Marketing plan refers to a road map for the marketing activities of an organization for a specified future period of time, such as one year or five years.
Marketing	Promoting and selling products or services to customers, or prospective customers, is referred to as marketing.
Body language	Body language is a broad term for forms of communication using body movements or gestures

	instead of, or in addition to, sounds, verbal language, or other forms of communication.
Transcript	A copy of writing is referred to as a transcript. It is the official record of proceedings in a trial or hearing.
Interest	In finance and economics, interest is the price paid by a borrower for the use of a lender's money. In other words, interest is the amount of paid to "rent" money for a period of time.
Chain of command	An unbroken line of authority that links all individuals in the organization and specifies who reports to whom is a chain of command. The concept of chain of command also implies that higher rank alone does not entitle a person to give commands.
Communication network	A communication network refer to networks that form spontaneously and naturally as the interactions among workers continue over time.
Leadership	Management merely consists of leadership applied to business situations; or in other words: management forms a sub-set of the broader process of leadership.
Manufacturing	Production of goods primarily by the application of labor and capital to raw materials and other intermediate inputs, in contrast to agriculture, mining, forestry, fishing, and services a manufacturing.
Firm	An organization that employs resources to produce a good or service for profit and owns and operates one or more plants is referred to as a firm.
Liaison	An individual who serves as a bridge between groups, tying groups together and facilitating the communication flow needed to integrate group activities is a liaison.
Production	The creation of finished goods and services using the factors of production: land, labor, capital, entrepreneurship, and knowledge.
Technology	The body of knowledge and techniques that can be used to combine economic resources to produce goods and services is called technology.
Stakeholder	A stakeholder is an individual or group with a vested interest in or expectation for organizational performance. Usually stakeholders can either have an effect on or are affected by an organization.
Drawback	Drawback refers to rebate of import duties when the imported good is re-exported or used as input to the production of an exported good.
Users	Users refer to people in the organization who actually use the product or service purchased by the buying center.
Empathy	Empathy refers to dimension of service quality-caring individualized attention provided to customers.
Closing	The finalization of a real estate sales transaction that passes title to the property from the seller to the buyer is referred to as a closing. Closing is a sales term which refers to the process of making a sale. It refers to reaching the final step, which may be an exchange of money or acquiring a signature.
Layoff	A layoff is the termination of an employee or (more commonly) a group of employees for business reasons, such as the decision that certain positions are no longer necessary.
Preparation	Preparation refers to usually the first stage in the creative process. It includes education and formal training.
Clutter	The nonprogram material that appears in a broadcast environment, including commercials, promotional messages for shows, public service announcements, and the like is called clutter.
Extranet	An extension of the Internet that connects suppliers, customers, and other organizations via

	secure websites is an extranet.
Intranet	Intranet refers to a companywide network, closed to public access, that uses Internet-type technology. A set of communications links within one company that travel over the Internet but are closed to public access.
Wholesale	According to the United Nations Statistics Division Wholesale is the resale of new and used goods to retailers, to industrial, commercial, institutional or professional users, or to other wholesalers, or involves acting as an agent or broker in buying merchandise for, or selling merchandise, to such persons or companies.
Extension	Extension refers to an out-of-court settlement in which creditors agree to allow the firm more time to meet its financial obligations. A new repayment schedule will be developed, subject to the acceptance of creditors.
Market	A market is, as defined in economics, a social arrangement that allows buyers and sellers to discover information and carry out a voluntary exchange of goods or services.
Telecommuting	Telecommuting is a work arrangement in which employees enjoy limited flexibility in working location and hours.
Inventory	Tangible property held for sale in the normal course of business or used in producing goods or services for sale is an inventory.
Organizational communication	Thee process by which information is exchanged in the organizational setting is organizational communication.
Organizational performance	Organizational performance comprises the actual output or results of an organization as measured against its intended outputs (or goals and objectives).
Knowledge management	Sharing, organizing and disseminating information in the simplest and most relevant way possible for the users of the information is a knowledge management.
Siemens	Siemens is the world's largest conglomerate company. Worldwide, Siemens and its subsidiaries employs 461,000 people (2005) in 190 countries and reported global sales of €75.4 billion in fiscal year 2005.
Bid	A bid price is a price offered by a buyer when he/she buys a good. In the context of stock trading on a stock exchange, the bid price is the highest price a buyer of a stock is willing to pay for a share of that given stock.
Cisco Systems	While Cisco Systems was not the first company to develop and sell a router (a device that forwards computer traffic from one network to another), it did create the first commercially successful multi-protocol router to allow previously incompatible computers to communicate using different network protocols.
Volkswagen	Volkswagen or VW is an automobile manufacturer based in Wolfsburg, Germany in the state of Lower Saxony. It forms the core of this Group, one of the world's four largest car producers. Its German tagline is "Aus Liebe zum Automobil", which is translated as "For the love of the car" - or, For Love of the People's Cars,".
Intel	Intel Corporation, founded in 1968 and based in Santa Clara, California, USA, is the world's largest semiconductor company. Intel is best known for its PC microprocessors, where it maintains roughly 80% market share.
Ford	Ford is an American company that manufactures and sells automobiles worldwide. Ford introduced methods for large-scale manufacturing of cars, and large-scale management of an industrial workforce, especially elaborately engineered manufacturing sequences typified by the moving assembly lines.
Financial assets	Financial assets refer to monetary claims or obligations by one party against another party.

	Examples are bonds, mortgages, bank loans, and equities.
Asset	An item of property, such as land, capital, money, a share in ownership, or a claim on others for future payment, such as a bond or a bank deposit is an asset.
Effective communication	When the intended meaning equals the perceived meaning it is called effective communication.
Distribution	Distribution in economics, the manner in which total output and income is distributed among individuals or factors.
Negotiation	Negotiation is the process whereby interested parties resolve disputes, agree upon courses of action, bargain for individual or collective advantage, and/or attempt to craft outcomes which serve their mutual interests.
Gain	In finance, gain is a profit or an increase in value of an investment such as a stock or bond. Gain is calculated by fair market value or the proceeds from the sale of the investment minus the sum of the purchase price and all costs associated with it.
Depression	Depression refers to a prolonged period characterized by high unemployment, low output and investment, depressed business confidence, falling prices, and widespread business failures. A milder form of business downturn is a recession.
Variable	A variable is something measured by a number; it is used to analyze what happens to other things when the size of that number changes.
Context	The effect of the background under which a message often takes on more and richer meaning is a context. Context is especially important in cross-cultural interactions because some cultures are said to be high context or low context.
Evaluation	The consumer's appraisal of the product or brand on important attributes is called evaluation.
Promotion	Promotion refers to all the techniques sellers use to motivate people to buy products or services. An attempt by marketers to inform people about products and to persuade them to participate in an exchange.
Performance appraisal	An evaluation in which the performance level of employees is measured against established standards to make decisions about promotions, compenzation, additional training, or firing is referred to as performance appraisal.
Jargon	Jargon is terminology, much like slang, that relates to a specific activity, profession, or group. It develops as a kind of shorthand, to express ideas that are frequently discussed between members of a group, and can also have the effect of distinguishing those belonging to a group from those who are not.
Active listening	Active listening is a way of "listening for meaning" in which the listener checks with the speaker to see that a statement has been correctly heard and understood. The goal of active listening is to improve mutual understanding.

Leadership	Management merely consists of leadership applied to business situations; or in other words: management forms a sub-set of the broader process of leadership.
Possession	Possession refers to respecting real property, exclusive dominion and control such as owners of like property usually exercise over it. Manual control of personal property either as owner or as one having a qualified right in it.
Trait theory	An approach to leadership that assumes leaders possess traits that make them fundamentally different from followers. Advocates of trait theory believe that some people have unique leadership characteristics and qualities that enable them to assume responsibilities not everyone can execute. Therefore they are 'born' leaders.
Charisma	A form of interpersonal attraction that inspires support and acceptance from others is charisma. It refers especially to a quality in certain people who easily draw the attention and admiration (or even hatred if the charisma is negative) of others due to a "magnetic" quality of personality and/or appearance.
Comprehensive	A comprehensive refers to a layout accurate in size, color, scheme, and other necessary details to show how a final ad will look. For presentation only, never for reproduction.
Conscientiou-ness	Conscientiousness is the trait of being painstaking and careful, or the quality of being in accord with the dictates of one's conscience.Conscientiousness includes traits such as self-discipline, carefulness, thoroughness, orderedness, deliberation (the tendency to think carefully before acting) and need for achievement.
Openness	Openness refers to the extent to which an economy is open, often measured by the ratio of its trade to GDP.
Trait approach	This approach attempted to identify stable and enduring character traits that differentiated effective leaders from nonleaders is called trait approach.
Behavioral approach	Behavioral approach refers to approach to leadership that tries to identify behaviors that differentiated effective leaders from nonleaders. It uses rules of thumb, suboptimizing, and satisfying in making decisions.
Supply	Supply is the aggregate amount of any material good that can be called into being at a certain price point; it comprises one half of the equation of supply and demand. In classical economic theory, a curve representing supply is one of the factors that produce price.
Consideration	Consideration in contract law, a basic requirement for an enforceable agreement under traditional contract principles, defined in this text as legal value, bargained for and given in exchange for an act or promise. In corporation law, cash or property contributed to a corporation in exchange for shares, or a promise to contribute such cash or property.
Production	The creation of finished goods and services using the factors of production: land, labor, capital, entrepreneurship, and knowledge.
Interest	In finance and economics, interest is the price paid by a borrower for the use of a lender's money. In other words, interest is the amount of paid to "rent" money for a period of time.
Job satisfaction	Job satisfaction describes how content an individual is with his or her job. It is a relatively recent term since in previous centuries the jobs available to a particular person were often predetermined by the occupation of that person's parent.
Productivity	Productivity refers to the total output of goods and services in a given period of time divided by work hours.
Managerial Grid	The Managerial Grid Model (1964) is a behavioral leadership model developed by Robert Blake and Jane Mouton. This model identifies five different leadership styles based on the concern for people and the concern for production.

Situational influences	The purchase situation affects the purchase decision process through five situational influences: the purchase task, social surroundings, physical surroundings, temporal effects, and antecedent states.
Contingency theory	Any theory that presupposes that there is no theory or method for operating a business that can be applied in all instances is referred to as a contingency theory.
Exchange	The trade of things of value between buyer and seller so that each is better off after the trade is called the exchange.
Instrument	Instrument refers to an economic variable that is controlled by policy makers and can be used to influence other variables, called targets. Examples are monetary and fiscal policies used to achieve external and internal balance.
Respondent	Respondent refers to a term often used to describe the party charged in an administrative proceeding. The party adverse to the appellant in a case appealed to a higher court.
Position power	Position power refers to power manager's hold due to their role in the organization. May include a manager's network of contacts, legitimate authority and control over information, rewards, punishments, and the work environment.
Assignment	A transfer of property or some right or interest is referred to as assignment.
Promotion	Promotion refers to all the techniques sellers use to motivate people to buy products or services. An attempt by marketers to inform people about products and to persuade them to participate in an exchange.
Variable	A variable is something measured by a number; it is used to analyze what happens to other things when the size of that number changes.
Trust	An arrangement in which shareholders of independent firms agree to give up their stock in exchange for trust certificates that entitle them to a share of the trust's common profits.
Assessment	Collecting information and providing feedback to employees about their behavior, communication style, or skills is an assessment.
Matching	Matching refers to an accounting concept that establishes when expenses are recognized. Expenses are matched with the revenues they helped to generate and are recognized when those revenues are recognized.
Foundation	A Foundation is a type of philanthropic organization set up by either individuals or institutions as a legal entity (either as a corporation or trust) with the purpose of distributing grants to support causes in line with the goals of the foundation.
Disparity	Disparity refers to the regional and economic differences in a country, province, state, or continent
Turnover	Turnover in a financial context refers to the rate at which a provider of goods cycles through its average inventory. Turnover in a human resources context refers to the characteristic of a given company or industry, relative to rate at which an employer gains and loses staff.
Expectancy theory	A process theory that proposes that motivation depends on individuals' expectations about their ability to perform tasks and receive desired rewards is called expectancy theory.
Directive leadership	Spells out the what and how of subordinates task and expects subordinates to follow orders is called directive leadership.
Supportive leadership	That which focuses on subordinate needs, well-being, and promotion of a friendly work climate is supportive leadership.
Internal locus	People tend to ascribe their chances of future successes or failures either to internal or

of control	external causes. Persons with an internal locus of control see themselves as responsible for the outcomes of their own actions.
External locus of control	The belief by individuals that their future is not within their control but rather is influenced by external forces is referred to as external locus of control.
Decision tree	In decision theory, a decision tree is a graph of decisions and their possible consequences, (including resource costs and risks) used to create a plan to reach a goal.
Apple Computer	Apple Computer has been a major player in the evolution of personal computing since its founding in 1976. The Apple II microcomputer, introduced in 1977, was a hit with home users.
Mary Kay Ash	Mary Kay Ash (May 12, 1908–November 22, 2001) was a U.S. businesswoman and the founder of one of the largest direct sellers of skin care and color cosmetics in the world.
Attribution	Under certain circumstances, the tax law applies attribution rules to assign to one taxpayer the ownership interest of another taxpayer.
Status quo	Status quo is a Latin term meaning the present, current, existing state of affairs.
Charismatic leader	A leader who has the ability to motivate subordinates to transcend their expected performance is a charismatic leader.
Correlation	A correlation is the measure of the extent to which two economic or statistical variables move together, normalized so that its values range from -1 to +1. It is defined as the covariance of the two variables divided by the square root of the product of their variances.
Firm	An organization that employs resources to produce a good or service for profit and owns and operates one or more plants is referred to as a firm.
Great Depression	The period of severe economic contraction and high unemployment that began in 1929 and continued throughout the 1930s is referred to as the Great Depression.
Depression	Depression refers to a prolonged period characterized by high unemployment, low output and investment, depressed business confidence, falling prices, and widespread business failures. A milder form of business downturn is a recession.
Bankruptcy	Bankruptcy is a legally declared inability or impairment of ability of an individual or organization to pay their creditors.
Supervisor	A Supervisor is an employee of an organization with some of the powers and responsibilities of management, occupying a role between true manager and a regular employee. A Supervisor position is typically the first step towards being promoted into a management role.
Peak	Peak refers to the point in the business cycle when an economic expansion reaches its highest point before turning down. Contrasts with trough.
Jack Welch	In 1986, GE acquired NBC. During the 90s, Jack Welch helped to modernize GE by emphasizing a shift from manufacturing to services. He also made hundreds of acquisitions and made a push to dominate markets abroad. Welch adopted the Six Sigma quality program in late 1995.
WorldCom	WorldCom was the United States' second largest long distance phone company (AT&T was the largest). WorldCom grew largely by acquiring other telecommunications companies, most notably MCI Communications. It also owned the Tier 1 ISP UUNET, a major part of the Internet backbone.
Disney	Disney is one of the largest media and entertainment corporations in the world. Founded on October 16, 1923 by brothers Walt and Roy Disney as a small animation studio, today it is one of the largest Hollywood studios and also owns nine theme parks and several television networks, including the American Broadcasting Company (ABC).
Enron	Enron Corportaion's global reputation was undermined by persistent rumours of bribery and

	political pressure to secure contracts in Central America, South America, Africa, and the Philippines. Especially controversial was its $3 billion contract with the Maharashtra State Electricity Board in India, where it is alleged that Enron officials used political connections within the Clinton and Bush administrations to exert pressure on the board.
Stock option	A stock option is a specific type of option that uses the stock itself as an underlying instrument to determine the option's pay-off and therefore its value.
Option	A contract that gives the purchaser the option to buy or sell the underlying financial instrument at a specified price, called the exercise price or strike price, within a specific period of time.
Stock	In financial terminology, stock is the capital raized by a corporation, through the issuance and sale of shares.
Emotional intelligence	The ability to understand one's own emotions and the emotions of people with whom one interacts on a daily basis is referred to as the emotional intelligence.
Empathy	Empathy refers to dimension of service quality-caring individualized attention provided to customers.
Management	Management characterizes the process of leading and directing all or part of an organization, often a business, through the deployment and manipulation of resources. Early twentieth-century management writer Mary Parker Follett defined management as "the art of getting things done through people."
Perjury	Perjury refers to the willful and corrupt false swearing or affirming, after an oath lawfully administered, in the course of a judicial or quasi-judicial proceeding, as to some matter material to the issue or point in question.
Hearing	A hearing is a proceeding before a court or other decision-making body or officer. A hearing is generally distinguished from a trial in that it is usually shorter and often less formal.
Competitor	Other organizations in the same industry or type of business that provide a good or service to the same set of customers is referred to as a competitor.
Subsidiary	A company that is controlled by another company or corporation is a subsidiary.
Microsoft	Microsoft is a multinational computer technology corporation with 2004 global annual sales of US$39.79 billion and 71,553 employees in 102 countries and regions as of July 2006. It develops, manufactures, licenses, and supports a wide range of software products for computing devices.
Participative leadership	Leadership style that consists of managers and employees working together to make decisions is referred to as participative leadership.
Power distance	Power distance refers to the degree to which the less powerful members of society expect there to be differences in the levels of power. A high score suggests that there is an expectation that some individuals wield larger amounts of power than others. Countries with high power distance rating are often characterized by a high rate of political violence.
Organizational Behavior	The study of human behavior in organizational settings, the interface between human behavior and the organization, and the organization itself is called organizational behavior.
Liability	A liability is a present obligation of the enterprise arizing from past events, the settlement of which is expected to result in an outflow from the enterprise of resources embodying economic benefits.
Inherent Risk	Inherent risk is the auditor's assessment that there are material misstatements in the financial statements before considering the effectiveness of internal controls. If the auditor concludes that there is a high likelihood of misstamtement, ignoring internal

	controls, the auditor would conclude that the inherent risk is high.
Loyalty	Marketers tend to define customer loyalty as making repeat purchases. Some argue that it should be defined attitudinally as a strongly positive feeling about the brand.
Profit	Profit refers to the return to the resource entrepreneurial ability; total revenue minus total cost.
Buyer	A buyer refers to a role in the buying center with formal authority and responsibility to select the supplier and negotiate the terms of the contract.
Authority	Authority in agency law, refers to an agent's ability to affect his principal's legal relations with third parties. Also used to refer to an actor's legal power or ability to do something. In addition, sometimes used to refer to a statute, case, or other legal source that justifies a particular result.
Bond	Bond refers to a debt instrument, issued by a borrower and promising a specified stream of payments to the purchaser, usually regular interest payments plus a final repayment of principal.
Contract	A contract is a "promise" or an "agreement" that is enforced or recognized by the law. In the civil law, a contract is considered to be part of the general law of obligations.
Context	The effect of the background under which a message often takes on more and richer meaning is a context. Context is especially important in cross-cultural interactions because some cultures are said to be high context or low context.
Agent	A person who makes economic decisions for another economic actor. A hired manager operates as an agent for a firm's owner.
Distribution	Distribution in economics, the manner in which total output and income is distributed among individuals or factors.
Equity	Equity is the name given to the set of legal principles, in countries following the English common law tradition, which supplement strict rules of law where their application would operate harshly, so as to achieve what is sometimes referred to as "natural justice."
Credit	Credit refers to a recording as positive in the balance of payments, any transaction that gives rise to a payment into the country, such as an export, the sale of an asset, or borrowing from abroad.
Performance appraisal	An evaluation in which the performance level of employees is measured against established standards to make decisions about promotions, compenzation, additional training, or firing is referred to as performance appraisal.
Interpersonal skills	Interpersonal skills are used to communicate with, understand, and motivate individuals and groups.
Contribution	In business organization law, the cash or property contributed to a business by its owners is referred to as contribution.
Senior executive	Senior executive means a chief executive officer, chief operating officer, chief financial officer and anyone in charge of a principal business unit or function.
Effective manager	Leader of a team that consistently achieves high performance goals is an effective manager.

Compatibility	Compatibility refers to used to describe a product characteristic, it means a good fit with other products used by the consumer or with the consumer's lifestyle. Used in a technical context, it means the ability of systems to work together.
Leadership	Management merely consists of leadership applied to business situations; or in other words: management forms a sub-set of the broader process of leadership.
Compliance	A type of influence process where a receiver accepts the position advocated by a source to obtain favorable outcomes or to avoid punishment is the compliance.
Authority	Authority in agency law, refers to an agent's ability to affect his principal's legal relations with third parties. Also used to refer to an actor's legal power or ability to do something. In addition, sometimes used to refer to a statute, case, or other legal source that justifies a particular result.
Coercive power	Coercive power refers to the extent to which a person has the ability to punish or physically or psychologically harm someone else.
Controlling	A management function that involves determining whether or not an organization is progressing toward its goals and objectives, and taking corrective action if it is not is called controlling.
Legitimate power	Legitimate power refers to power that is granted by virtue of one's position in the organization.
Principal	In agency law, one under whose direction an agent acts and for whose benefit that agent acts is a principal.
Profit	Profit refers to the return to the resource entrepreneurial ability; total revenue minus total cost.
Intel	Intel Corporation, founded in 1968 and based in Santa Clara, California, USA, is the world's largest semiconductor company. Intel is best known for its PC microprocessors, where it maintains roughly 80% market share.
Expert power	The extent to which a person controls information that is valuable to someone else is referred to as expert power.
Referent power	Referent power is individual power based on a high level of identification with, admiration of, or respect for the powerholder.
Marketing research	Marketing research refers to the analysis of markets to determine opportunities and challenges, and to find the information needed to make good decisions.
Marketing	Promoting and selling products or services to customers, or prospective customers, is referred to as marketing.
Charisma	A form of interpersonal attraction that inspires support and acceptance from others is charisma. It refers especially to a quality in certain people who easily draw the attention and admiration (or even hatred if the charisma is negative) of others due to a "magnetic" quality of personality and/or appearance.
Extension	Extension refers to an out-of-court settlement in which creditors agree to allow the firm more time to meet its financial obligations. A new repayment schedule will be developed, subject to the acceptance of creditors.
Gain	In finance, gain is a profit or an increase in value of an investment such as a stock or bond. Gain is calculated by fair market value or the proceeds from the sale of the investment minus the sum of the purchase price and all costs associated with it.
Supply	Supply is the aggregate amount of any material good that can be called into being at a

	certain price point; it comprises one half of the equation of supply and demand. In classical economic theory, a curve representing supply is one of the factors that produce price.
Possession	Possession refers to respecting real property, exclusive dominion and control such as owners of like property usually exercise over it. Manual control of personal property either as owner or as one having a qualified right in it.
Scarcity	Scarcity is defined as not having sufficient resources to produce enough to fulfill unlimited subjective wants. Alternatively, scarcity implies that not all of society's goals can be attained at the same time, so that trade-offs one good against others are made.
Personnel	A collective term for all of the employees of an organization. Personnel is also commonly used to refer to the personnel management function or the organizational unit responsible for administering personnel programs.
Accounting	A system that collects and processes financial information about an organization and reports that information to decision makers is referred to as accounting.
Market	A market is, as defined in economics, a social arrangement that allows buyers and sellers to discover information and carry out a voluntary exchange of goods or services.
Bargaining power	Bargaining power refers to the ability to influence the setting of prices or wages, usually arising from some sort of monopoly or monopsony position
Coalition	An informal alliance among managers who support a specific goal is called coalition.
Holder	A person in possession of a document of title or an instrument payable or indorsed to him, his order, or to bearer is a holder.
Expense	In accounting, an expense represents an event in which an asset is used up or a liability is incurred. In terms of the accounting equation, expenses reduce owners' equity.
Labor union	A group of workers organized to advance the interests of the group is called a labor union.
Management	Management characterizes the process of leading and directing all or part of an organization, often a business, through the deployment and manipulation of resources. Early twentieth-century management writer Mary Parker Follett defined management as "the art of getting things done through people."
Labor	People's physical and mental talents and efforts that are used to help produce goods and services are called labor.
Union	A worker association that bargains with employers over wages and working conditions is called a union.
Security	Security refers to a claim on the borrower future income that is sold by the borrower to the lender. A security is a type of transferable interest representing financial value.
Wage	The payment for the service of a unit of labor, per unit time. In trade theory, it is the only payment to labor, usually unskilled labor. In empirical work, wage data may exclude other compenzation, which must be added to get the total cost of employment.
Interest	In finance and economics, interest is the price paid by a borrower for the use of a lender's money. In other words, interest is the amount of paid to "rent" money for a period of time.
Organizational culture	The mindset of employees, including their shared beliefs, values, and goals is called the organizational culture.
Interdependence	The extent to which departments depend on each other for resources or materials to accomplish their tasks is referred to as interdependence.
Sexual	Unwelcome sexual advances, requests for sexual favors, and other conduct of a sexual nature

harassment	is called sexual harassment.
Philip Morris	Philip Morris, is the world's largest commercial tobacco company by sales. Philip Morris was begun by a London tobacconist of the same name. He was one of the first people to sell hand-rolled cigarettes in the 1860s, selling them under the brand names Oxford and Cambridge Blues, following the adoption of cigarette smoking by British soldiers returning from the Crimean War.
Supervisor	A Supervisor is an employee of an organization with some of the powers and responsibilities of management, occupying a role between true manager and a regular employee. A Supervisor position is typically the first step towards being promoted into a management role.
Jury	A body of lay persons, selected by lot, or by some other fair and impartial means, to ascertain, under the guidance of the judge, the truth in questions of fact arising either in civil litigation or a criminal process is referred to as jury.
Retaliation	The use of an increased trade barrier in response to another country increasing its trade barrier, either as a way of undoing the adverse effects of the latter's action or of punishing it is retaliation.
Niche	In industry, a niche is a situation or an activity perfectly suited to a person. A niche can imply a working position or an area suited to a person who occupies it. Basically, a job where a person is able to succeed and thrive.
Organizational politics	Organizational politics occurs when power sources and influence tactics are used to serve personal goals or motives.
Cooperative	A business owned and controlled by the people who use it, producers, consumers, or workers with similar needs who pool their resources for mutual gain is called cooperative.
Internal environment	Variables that are under some degree of control by organizational members is the internal enviroment. Internal environment scans are conducted to identify an organization's internal capabilities, performance levels, strengths, and weaknesses.
Internal locus of control	People tend to ascribe their chances of future successes or failures either to internal or external causes. Persons with an internal locus of control see themselves as responsible for the outcomes of their own actions.
Variable	A variable is something measured by a number; it is used to analyze what happens to other things when the size of that number changes.
Promotion	Promotion refers to all the techniques sellers use to motivate people to buy products or services. An attempt by marketers to inform people about products and to persuade them to participate in an exchange.
Trust	An arrangement in which shareholders of independent firms agree to give up their stock in exchange for trust certificates that entitle them to a share of the trust's common profits.
Role ambiguity	Uncertainty of specifications for a role is role ambiguity. This occurs when duties for a role are not specified. The resolution to role ambiguity may lie in precise role descriptions (job descriptions) or a simplification of the tasks.
Scope	Scope of a project is the sum total of all projects products and their requirements or features.
Evaluation	The consumer's appraisal of the product or brand on important attributes is called evaluation.
Committee	A long-lasting, sometimes permanent team in the organization structure created to deal with tasks that recur regularly is the committee.

Productivity	Productivity refers to the total output of goods and services in a given period of time divided by work hours.
Pleading	In the law, a pleading is one of the papers filed with a court in a civil action, such as a complaint, a demurrer, or an answer.
Distortion	Distortion refers to any departure from the ideal of perfect competition that interferes with economic agents maximizing social welfare when they maximize their own.
Deception	According to the Federal Trade Commission, a misrepresentation, omission, or practice that is likely to mislead the consumer acting reasonably in the circumstances to the consumer's detriment is referred to as deception.
Distribution	Distribution in economics, the manner in which total output and income is distributed among individuals or factors.
Context	The effect of the background under which a message often takes on more and richer meaning is a context. Context is especially important in cross-cultural interactions because some cultures are said to be high context or low context.
Misrepresent-tion	The assertion of a fact that is not in accord with the truth is misrepresentation. A contract can be rescinded on the ground of misrepresentation when the assertion relates to a material fact or is made fraudulently and the other party actually and justifiably relies on the assertion.
Assessment	Collecting information and providing feedback to employees about their behavior, communication style, or skills is an assessment.
Applicant	In many tribunal and administrative law suits, the person who initiates the claim is called the applicant.
Equity	Equity is the name given to the set of legal principles, in countries following the English common law tradition, which supplement strict rules of law where their application would operate harshly, so as to achieve what is sometimes referred to as "natural justice."
Effective manager	Leader of a team that consistently achieves high performance goals is an effective manager.

Openness	Openness refers to the extent to which an economy is open, often measured by the ratio of its trade to GDP.
Trust	An arrangement in which shareholders of independent firms agree to give up their stock in exchange for trust certificates that entitle them to a share of the trust's common profits.
Organizational performance	Organizational performance comprises the actual output or results of an organization as measured against its intended outputs (or goals and objectives).
Contribution	In business organization law, the cash or property contributed to a business by its owners is referred to as contribution.
Dysfunctional conflict	Conflict that is responsible for hindering group performance is dysfunctional conflict.
Personalization	The consumer-initiated practice of generating content on a marketer's website that is custom tailored to an individual's specific needs and preferences is called personalization.
Collaboration	Collaboration occurs when the interaction between groups is very important to goal attainment and the goals are compatible. Wherein people work together —applying both to the work of individuals as well as larger collectives and societies.
Accommodation	Accommodation is a term used to describe a delivery of nonconforming goods meant as a partial performance of a contract for the sale of goods, where a full performance is not possible.
Compromise	Compromise occurs when the interaction is moderately important to meeting goals and the goals are neither completely compatible nor completely incompatible.
Variable	A variable is something measured by a number; it is used to analyze what happens to other things when the size of that number changes.
Channel	Channel, in communications (sometimes called communications channel), refers to the medium used to convey information from a sender (or transmitter) to a receiver.
Communication channel	The pathways through which messages are communicated are called a communication channel.
Communication network	A communication network refer to networks that form spontaneously and naturally as the interactions among workers continue over time.
Exchange	The trade of things of value between buyer and seller so that each is better off after the trade is called the exchange.
Foundation	A Foundation is a type of philanthropic organization set up by either individuals or institutions as a legal entity (either as a corporation or trust) with the purpose of distributing grants to support causes in line with the goals of the foundation.
Standardization	Standardization, in the context related to technologies and industries, is the process of establishing a technical standard among competing entities in a market, where this will bring benefits without hurting competition.
Leadership	Management merely consists of leadership applied to business situations; or in other words: management forms a sub-set of the broader process of leadership.
Context	The effect of the background under which a message often takes on more and richer meaning is a context. Context is especially important in cross-cultural interactions because some cultures are said to be high context or low context.
Turnover	Turnover in a financial context refers to the rate at which a provider of goods cycles through its average inventory. Turnover in a human resources context refers to the characteristic of a given company or industry, relative to rate at which an employer gains and loses staff.

Promotion	Promotion refers to all the techniques sellers use to motivate people to buy products or services. An attempt by marketers to inform people about products and to persuade them to participate in an exchange.
Value system	A value system refers to how an individual or a group of individuals organize their ethical or ideological values. A well-defined value system is a moral code.
Assessment	Collecting information and providing feedback to employees about their behavior, communication style, or skills is an assessment.
Prejudice	Prejudice is, as the name implies, the process of "pre-judging" something. It implies coming to a judgment on a subject before learning where the preponderance of evidence actually lies, or forming a judgment without direct experience.
Interest	In finance and economics, interest is the price paid by a borrower for the use of a lender's money. In other words, interest is the amount of paid to "rent" money for a period of time.
Strike	The withholding of labor services by an organized group of workers is referred to as a strike.
Points	Loan origination fees that may be deductible as interest by a buyer of property. A seller of property who pays points reduces the selling price by the amount of the points paid for the buyer.
Interdependence	The extent to which departments depend on each other for resources or materials to accomplish their tasks is referred to as interdependence.
Negotiation	Negotiation is the process whereby interested parties resolve disputes, agree upon courses of action, bargain for individual or collective advantage, and/or attempt to craft outcomes which serve their mutual interests.
Management	Management characterizes the process of leading and directing all or part of an organization, often a business, through the deployment and manipulation of resources. Early twentieth-century management writer Mary Parker Follett defined management as "the art of getting things done through people."
Contract	A contract is a "promise" or an "agreement" that is enforced or recognized by the law. In the civil law, a contract is considered to be part of the general law of obligations.
Labor	People's physical and mental talents and efforts that are used to help produce goods and services are called labor.
Union	A worker association that bargains with employers over wages and working conditions is called a union.
Uncertainty avoidance	The extent to which people prefer to be in clear and unambiguous situations is referred to as the uncertainty avoidance.
Innovation	Innovation refers to the first commercially successful introduction of a new product, the use of a new method of production, or the creation of a new form of business organization.
Consideration	Consideration in contract law, a basic requirement for an enforceable agreement under traditional contract principles, defined in this text as legal value, bargained for and given in exchange for an act or promise. In corporation law, cash or property contributed to a corporation in exchange for shares, or a promise to contribute such cash or property.
Status quo	Status quo is a Latin term meaning the present, current, existing state of affairs.
Homogeneous	In the context of procurement/purchasing, homogeneous is used to describe goods that do not vary in their essential characteristic irrespective of the source of supply.
Brand	A name, symbol, or design that identifies the goods or services of one seller or group of

	sellers and distinguishes them from the goods and services of competitors is a brand.
Advertising	Advertising refers to paid, nonpersonal communication through various media by organizations and individuals who are in some way identified in the advertising message.
Stock	In financial terminology, stock is the capital raized by a corporation, through the issuance and sale of shares.
Peak	Peak refers to the point in the business cycle when an economic expansion reaches its highest point before turning down. Contrasts with trough.
Administration	Administration refers to the management and direction of the affairs of governments and institutions; a collective term for all policymaking officials of a government; the execution and implementation of public policy.
Groupthink	Groupthink is a situation in which pressures for cohesion and togetherness are so strong as to produce narrowly considered and bad decisions; this can be especially true via conformity pressures in groups.
Policy	Similar to a script in that a policy can be a less than completely rational decision-making method. Involves the use of a pre-existing set of decision steps for any problem that presents itself.
Productivity	Productivity refers to the total output of goods and services in a given period of time divided by work hours.
Research and development	The use of resources for the deliberate discovery of new information and ways of doing things, together with the application of that information in inventing new products or processes is referred to as research and development.
Analyst	Analyst refers to a person or tool with a primary function of information analysis, generally with a more limited, practical and short term set of goals than a researcher.
Economic problem	Economic problem refers to how to determine the use of scarce resources among competing uses. Because resources are scarce, the economy must choose what products to produce; how these products are to be produced: and for whom.
Consultant	A professional that provides expert advice in a particular field or area in which customers occassionaly require this type of knowledge is a consultant.
Corporation	A legal entity chartered by a state or the Federal government that is distinct and separate from the individuals who own it is a corporation. This separation gives the corporation unique powers which other legal entities lack.
Mistake	In contract law a mistake is incorrect understanding by one or more parties to a contract and may be used as grounds to invalidate the agreement. Common law has identified three different types of mistake in contract: unilateral mistake, mutual mistake, and common mistake.
General Electric	In 1876, Thomas Alva Edison opened a new laboratory in Menlo Park, New Jersey. Out of the laboratory was to come perhaps the most famous invention of all—a successful development of the incandescent electric lamp. By 1890, Edison had organized his various businesses into the Edison General Electric Company.
Shell	One of the original Seven Sisters, Royal Dutch/Shell is the world's third-largest oil company by revenue, and a major player in the petrochemical industry and the solar energy business. Shell has six core businesses: Exploration and Production, Gas and Power, Downstream, Chemicals, Renewables, and Trading/Shipping, and operates in more than 140 countries.
Purchasing	Purchasing refers to the function in a firm that searches for quality material resources, finds the best suppliers, and negotiates the best price for goods and services.

Agent	A person who makes economic decisions for another economic actor. A hired manager operates as an agent for a firm's owner.
Authority	Authority in agency law, refers to an agent's ability to affect his principal's legal relations with third parties. Also used to refer to an actor's legal power or ability to do something. In addition, sometimes used to refer to a statute, case, or other legal source that justifies a particular result.
Distributive bargaining	Distributive bargaining is the approach to bargaining or negotiation that is used when the parties are trying to divide something up--distribute something.
Wage	The payment for the service of a unit of labor, per unit time. In trade theory, it is the only payment to labor, usually unskilled labor. In empirical work, wage data may exclude other compenzation, which must be added to get the total cost of employment.
Tactic	A short-term immediate decision that, in its totality, leads to the achievement of strategic goals is called a tactic.
Integrative bargaining	The part of the labor-management negotiation process that seeks solutions beneficial to both sides is called integrative bargaining.
Credit	Credit refers to a recording as positive in the balance of payments, any transaction that gives rise to a payment into the country, such as an export, the sale of an asset, or borrowing from abroad.
Firm	An organization that employs resources to produce a good or service for profit and owns and operates one or more plants is referred to as a firm.
Organizational culture	The mindset of employees, including their shared beliefs, values, and goals is called the organizational culture.
Expense	In accounting, an expense represents an event in which an asset is used up or a liability is incurred. In terms of the accounting equation, expenses reduce owners' equity.
Gain	In finance, gain is a profit or an increase in value of an investment such as a stock or bond. Gain is calculated by fair market value or the proceeds from the sale of the investment minus the sum of the purchase price and all costs associated with it.
Option	A contract that gives the purchaser the option to buy or sell the underlying financial instrument at a specified price, called the exercise price or strike price, within a specific period of time.
Incentive	An incentive is any factor (financial or non-financial) that provides a motive for a particular course of action, or counts as a reason for preferring one choice to the alternatives.
Cooperative	A business owned and controlled by the people who use it, producers, consumers, or workers with similar needs who pool their resources for mutual gain is called cooperative.
Forming	The first stage of team development, where the team is formed and the objectives for the team are set is referred to as forming.
Anticipation	In finance, anticipation is where debts are paid off early, generally in order to pay less interest.
Direct relationship	Direct relationship refers to the relationship between two variables that change in the same direction, for example, product price and quantity supplied.
Final settlement	Final settlement occurs when the payor bank pays the check in cash, settles for the check without having a right to revoke the settlement, or fails to dishonor the check within certain statutory time periods.

Preparation

Preparation refers to usually the first stage in the creative process. It includes education and formal training.

Argument

The discussion by counsel for the respective parties of their contentions on the law and the facts of the case being tried in order to aid the jury in arriving at a correct and just conclusion is called argument.

Concession

A concession is a business operated under a contract or license associated with a degree of exclusivity in exploiting a business within a certain geographical area. For example, sports arenas or public parks may have concession stands; and public services such as water supply may be operated as concessions.

Concealment

In contract law, taking active steps to prevent another from learning the truth is referred to as concealment.

Organization structure	The system of task, reporting, and authority relationships within which the organization does its work is referred to as the organization structure.
Assembly line	An assembly line is a manufacturing process in which interchangeable parts are added to a product in a sequential manner to create a finished product.
Henry Ford	Henry Ford was the founder of the Ford Motor Company. His introduction of the Model T automobile revolutionized transportation and American industry.
Ford	Ford is an American company that manufactures and sells automobiles worldwide. Ford introduced methods for large-scale manufacturing of cars, and large-scale management of an industrial workforce, especially elaborately engineered manufacturing sequences typified by the moving assembly lines.
Work specialization	Work specialization refers to the degree to which organizational tasks are subdivided into individual jobs; also called division of labor.
Division of labor	Division of labor is generally speaking the specialization of cooperative labor in specific, circumscribed tasks and roles, intended to increase efficiency of output.
Labor	People's physical and mental talents and efforts that are used to help produce goods and services are called labor.
Manufacturing	Production of goods primarily by the application of labor and capital to raw materials and other intermediate inputs, in contrast to agriculture, mining, forestry, fishing, and services a manufacturing.
Management	Management characterizes the process of leading and directing all or part of an organization, often a business, through the deployment and manipulation of resources. Early twentieth-century management writer Mary Parker Follett defined management as "the art of getting things done through people."
Chain of command	An unbroken line of authority that links all individuals in the organization and specifies who reports to whom is a chain of command. The concept of chain of command also implies that higher rank alone does not entitle a person to give commands.
Decentralization	Decentralization is the process of redistributing decision-making closer to the point of service or action. This gives freedom to managers at lower levels of the organization to make decisions.
Span of control	Span of control refers to the optimum number of subordinates a manager supervises or should supervise.
Centralization	A structural policy in which decision-making authority is concentrated at the top of the organizational hierarchy is referred to as centralization.
Departmental-zation	The dividing of organizational functions into separate units is called departmentalization.
Productivity	Productivity refers to the total output of goods and services in a given period of time divided by work hours.
Accounting	A system that collects and processes financial information about an organization and reports that information to decision makers is referred to as accounting.
Specialist	A specialist is a trader who makes a market in one or several stocks and holds the limit order book for those stocks.
Purchasing	Purchasing refers to the function in a firm that searches for quality material resources, finds the best suppliers, and negotiates the best price for goods and services.
Personnel	A collective term for all of the employees of an organization. Personnel is also commonly

used to refer to the personnel management function or the organizational unit responsible for administering personnel programs.

Economies of scale — In economics, returns to scale and economies of scale are related terms that describe what happens as the scale of production increases. They are different terms and not to be used interchangeably.

Economy — The income, expenditures, and resources that affect the cost of running a business and household are called an economy.

Authority — Authority in agency law, refers to an agent's ability to affect his principal's legal relations with third parties. Also used to refer to an actor's legal power or ability to do something. In addition, sometimes used to refer to a statute, case, or other legal source that justifies a particular result.

Service — Service refers to a "non tangible product" that is not embodied in a physical good and that typically effects some change in another product, person, or institution. Contrasts with good.

Production — The creation of finished goods and services using the factors of production: land, labor, capital, entrepreneurship, and knowledge.

Alcoa — Alcoa (NYSE: AA) is the world's leading producer of alumina, primary and fabricated aluminum, with operations in 43 countries. (It is followed in this by a former subsidiary, Alcan, the second-leading producer.)

Categorizing — The act of placing strengths and weaknesses into categories in generic internal assessment is called categorizing.

Homogeneous — In the context of procurement/purchasing, homogeneous is used to describe goods that do not vary in their essential characteristic irrespective of the source of supply.

Wholesale — According to the United Nations Statistics Division Wholesale is the resale of new and used goods to retailers, to industrial, commercial, institutional or professional users, or to other wholesalers, or involves acting as an agent or broker in buying merchandise for, or selling merchandise, to such persons or companies.

Supply — Supply is the aggregate amount of any material good that can be called into being at a certain price point; it comprises one half of the equation of supply and demand. In classical economic theory, a curve representing supply is one of the factors that produce price.

Firm — An organization that employs resources to produce a good or service for profit and owns and operates one or more plants is referred to as a firm.

Trend — Trend refers to the long-term movement of an economic variable, such as its average rate of increase or decrease over enough years to encompass several business cycles.

Organizational design — The structuring of workers so that they can best accomplish the firm's goals is referred to as organizational design.

Technology — The body of knowledge and techniques that can be used to combine economic resources to produce goods and services is called technology.

Hierarchy — A system of grouping people in an organization according to rank from the top down in which all subordinate managers must report to one person is called a hierarchy.

Decentralized organization — An organization in which decision making is spread throughout the organization, rather than confined to a small group of executives is a decentralized organization.

Standardization — Standardization, in the context related to technologies and industries, is the process of establishing a technical standard among competing entities in a market, where this will bring

	benefits without hurting competition.
Flat organization	Flat organization refers to a organizational structure with few or no levels of intervening management between staff and managers. The idea is that well-trained workers will be more productive when they are more directly involved in the decision making process, rather than closely supervized by many layers of management.
Standstill	Standstill refers to a commitment to refrain from introducing new measures such as trade barriers that are not consistent with an agreement. Such commitments are usually offered at the start of multilateral trade negotiations as an indication of good faith.
Bureaucracy	Bureaucracy refers to an organization with many layers of managers who set rules and regulations and oversee all decisions.
Regulation	Regulation refers to restrictions state and federal laws place on business with regard to the conduct of its activities.
Centralized authority	An organization structure in which decision-making authority is maintained at the top level of management at the company's headquarters is a centralized authority.
Operation	A standardized method or technique that is performed repetitively, often on different materials resulting in different finished goods is called an operation.
Senior executive	Senior executive means a chief executive officer, chief operating officer, chief financial officer and anyone in charge of a principal business unit or function.
Decision rule	Decision rule refers to a statement that tells a decision maker which alternative to choose based on the characteristics of the decision situation.
Peak	Peak refers to the point in the business cycle when an economic expansion reaches its highest point before turning down. Contrasts with trough.
General Electric	In 1876, Thomas Alva Edison opened a new laboratory in Menlo Park, New Jersey. Out of the laboratory was to come perhaps the most famous invention of all—a successful development of the incandescent electric lamp. By 1890, Edison had organized his various businesses into the Edison General Electric Company.
Corporation	A legal entity chartered by a state or the Federal government that is distinct and separate from the individuals who own it is a corporation. This separation gives the corporation unique powers which other legal entities lack.
Volkswagen	Volkswagen or VW is an automobile manufacturer based in Wolfsburg, Germany in the state of Lower Saxony. It forms the core of this Group, one of the world's four largest car producers. Its German tagline is "Aus Liebe zum Automobil", which is translated as "For the love of the car" - or, For Love of the People's Cars,".
Shell	One of the original Seven Sisters, Royal Dutch/Shell is the world's third-largest oil company by revenue, and a major player in the petrochemical industry and the solar energy business. Shell has six core businesses: Exploration and Production, Gas and Power, Downstream, Chemicals, Renewables, and Trading/Shipping, and operates in more than 140 countries.
Matrix structure	An organizational structure which typically crosses a functional approach with a product or service-based design, often resulting in employees having two bosses is the matrix structure.
Option	A contract that gives the purchaser the option to buy or sell the underlying financial instrument at a specified price, called the exercise price or strike price, within a specific period of time.
Budget	Budget refers to an account, usually for a year, of the planned expenditures and the expected receipts of an entity. For a government, the receipts are tax revenues.

Gain	In finance, gain is a profit or an increase in value of an investment such as a stock or bond. Gain is calculated by fair market value or the proceeds from the sale of the investment minus the sum of the purchase price and all costs associated with it.
Product manager	Product manager refers to a person who plans, implements, and controls the annual and long-range plans for the products for which he or she is responsible.
Marketing	Promoting and selling products or services to customers, or prospective customers, is referred to as marketing.
Complexity	The technical sophistication of the product and hence the amount of understanding required to use it is referred to as complexity. It is the opposite of simplicity.
Efficient allocation	An allocation that it is impossible unambiguously to improve upon, in the sense of producing more of one good without producing less of another is an efficient allocation.
Role ambiguity	Uncertainty of specifications for a role is role ambiguity. This occurs when duties for a role are not specified. The resolution to role ambiguity may lie in precise role descriptions (job descriptions) or a simplification of the tasks.
Role conflict	Role conflict is a special form of social conflict that takes place when one is forced to take on two different and incompatible roles at the same time.
Core	A core is the set of feasible allocations in an economy that cannot be improved upon by subset of the set of the economy's consumers (a coalition). In construction, when the force in an element is within a certain center section, the core, the element will only be under compression.
Virtual organization	A temporary alliance between two or more organizations that band together to undertake a specific venture is a virtual organization.
Prototype	A prototype is built to test the function of a new design before starting production of a product.
Investment	Investment refers to spending for the production and accumulation of capital and additions to inventories. In a financial sense, buying an asset with the expectation of making a return.
Cisco Systems	While Cisco Systems was not the first company to develop and sell a router (a device that forwards computer traffic from one network to another), it did create the first commercially successful multi-protocol router to allow previously incompatible computers to communicate using different network protocols.
Nike	Because Nike creates goods for a wide range of sports, they have competition from every sports and sports fashion brand there is. Nike has no direct competitors because there is no single brand which can compete directly with their range of sports and non-sports oriented gear, except for Reebok.
Research and development	The use of resources for the deliberate discovery of new information and ways of doing things, together with the application of that information in inventing new products or processes is referred to as research and development.
ExxonMobil	ExxonMobil is the largest publicly traded integrated oil and gas company in the world, formed on November 30, 1999, by the merger of Exxon and Mobil. It is the sixth-largest company in the world as ranked by the Forbes Global 2000 and the largest company in the world (by revenue) as ranked by the Fortune Global 500.
Contract	A contract is a "promise" or an "agreement" that is enforced or recognized by the law. In the civil law, a contract is considered to be part of the general law of obligations.
Credit	Credit refers to a recording as positive in the balance of payments, any transaction that gives rise to a payment into the country, such as an export, the sale of an asset, or

	borrowing from abroad.
Controlling	A management function that involves determining whether or not an organization is progressing toward its goals and objectives, and taking corrective action if it is not is called controlling.
Drawback	Drawback refers to rebate of import duties when the imported good is re-exported or used as input to the production of an exported good.
Boundaryless organization	A boundaryless organization is an organization not defined or limited by horizontal, vertical, or external boundaries imposed by a predetermined structure. Similar to flat organizations, there is a strong emphasis on teams. Cross-functional teams dissolve horizontal barriers and enable the organization to respond quickly to environmental changes and to spearhead innovation.
Jack Welch	In 1986, GE acquired NBC. During the 90s, Jack Welch helped to modernize GE by emphasizing a shift from manufacturing to services. He also made hundreds of acquisitions and made a push to dominate markets abroad. Welch adopted the Six Sigma quality program in late 1995.
Revenue	Revenue is a U.S. business term for the amount of money that a company receives from its activities, mostly from sales of products and/or services to customers.
Hearing	A hearing is a proceeding before a court or other decision-making body or officer. A hearing is generally distinguished from a trial in that it is usually shorter and often less formal.
Aid	Assistance provided by countries and by international institutions such as the World Bank to developing countries in the form of monetary grants, loans at low interest rates, in kind, or a combination of these is called aid. Aid can also refer to assistance of any type rendered to benefit some group or individual.
Strategic alliance	Strategic alliance refers to a long-term partnership between two or more companies established to help each company build competitive market advantages.
Apple Computer	Apple Computer has been a major player in the evolution of personal computing since its founding in 1976. The Apple II microcomputer, introduced in 1977, was a hit with home users.
Partnership	In the common law, a partnership is a type of business entity in which partners share with each other the profits or losses of the business undertaking in which they have all invested.
Boeing	Boeing is the world's largest aircraft manufacturer by revenue. Headquartered in Chicago, Illinois, Boeing is the second-largest defense contractor in the world. In 2005, the company was the world's largest civil aircraft manufacturer in terms of value.
Intranet	Intranet refers to a companywide network, closed to public access, that uses Internet-type technology. A set of communications links within one company that travel over the Internet but are closed to public access.
Downward communication	Downward communication refers to communication flows from a company or boss down to the affected employees.
Innovation	Innovation refers to the first commercially successful introduction of a new product, the use of a new method of production, or the creation of a new form of business organization.
Expense	In accounting, an expense represents an event in which an asset is used up or a liability is incurred. In terms of the accounting equation, expenses reduce owners' equity.
Organic structure	Organic structure refers to an organizational form in which formality is low, power is decentralized and jobs are less specialized and are often broadly defined. Adaptability and flexibility in the face of rapidly changing conditions are usually the primary goals with such structures.

Inputs — The inputs used by a firm or an economy are the labor, raw materials, electricity and other resources it uses to produce its outputs.

Physical resources — Natural resources used in the transformation process to create resources of more value are called physical resources.

Security — Security refers to a claim on the borrower future income that is sold by the borrower to the lender. A security is a type of transferable interest representing financial value.

Organizational culture	The mindset of employees, including their shared beliefs, values, and goals is called the organizational culture.
Job satisfaction	Job satisfaction describes how content an individual is with his or her job. It is a relatively recent term since in previous centuries the jobs available to a particular person were often predetermined by the occupation of that person's parent.
Subculture	A subgroups within the larger, or national, culture with unique values, ideas, and attitudes is a subculture.
Property	Assets defined in the broadest legal sense. Property includes the unrealized receivables of a cash basis taxpayer, but not services rendered.
Core	A core is the set of feasible allocations in an economy that cannot be improved upon by subset of the set of the economy's consumers (a coalition). In construction, when the force in an element is within a certain center section, the core, the element will only be under compression.
Accounting	A system that collects and processes financial information about an organization and reports that information to decision makers is referred to as accounting.
Variable	A variable is something measured by a number; it is used to analyze what happens to other things when the size of that number changes.
Argument	The discussion by counsel for the respective parties of their contentions on the law and the facts of the case being tried in order to aid the jury in arriving at a correct and just conclusion is called argument.
Turnover	Turnover in a financial context refers to the rate at which a provider of goods cycles through its average inventory. Turnover in a human resources context refers to the characteristic of a given company or industry, relative to rate at which an employer gains and loses staff.
Disney	Disney is one of the largest media and entertainment corporations in the world. Founded on October 16, 1923 by brothers Walt and Roy Disney as a small animation studio, today it is one of the largest Hollywood studios and also owns nine theme parks and several television networks, including the American Broadcasting Company (ABC).
Liability	A liability is a present obligation of the enterprise arizing from past events, the settlement of which is expected to result in an outflow from the enterprise of resources embodying economic benefits.
Organizational commitment	A person's identification with and attachment to an organization is called organizational commitment.
Asset	An item of property, such as land, capital, money, a share in ownership, or a claim on others for future payment, such as a bond or a bank deposit is an asset.
Customs	Customs is an authority or agency in a country responsible for collecting customs duties and for controlling the flow of people, animals and goods (including personal effects and hazardous items) in and out of the country.
Conglomerate	A conglomerate is a large company that consists of divisions of often seemingly unrelated businesses.
Promotion	Promotion refers to all the techniques sellers use to motivate people to buy products or services. An attempt by marketers to inform people about products and to persuade them to participate in an exchange.
Performance appraisal	An evaluation in which the performance level of employees is measured against established standards to make decisions about promotions, compenzation, additional training, or firing is

	referred to as performance appraisal.
Socialization	Socialization is the process by which human beings or animals learn to adopt the behavior patterns of the community in which they live. For both humans and animals, this is typically thought to occur during the early stages of life, during which individuals develop the skills and knowledge necessary to function within their culture and environment.
Management	Management characterizes the process of leading and directing all or part of an organization, often a business, through the deployment and manipulation of resources. Early twentieth-century management writer Mary Parker Follett defined management as "the art of getting things done through people."
Applicant	In many tribunal and administrative law suits, the person who initiates the claim is called the applicant.
Teamwork	That which occurs when group members work together in ways that utilize their skills well to accomplish a purpose is called teamwork.
Senior executive	Senior executive means a chief executive officer, chief operating officer, chief financial officer and anyone in charge of a principal business unit or function.
Market value	Market value refers to the price of an asset agreed on between a willing buyer and a willing seller; the price an asset could demand if it is sold on the open market.
Market	A market is, as defined in economics, a social arrangement that allows buyers and sellers to discover information and carry out a voluntary exchange of goods or services.
Stock	In financial terminology, stock is the capital raized by a corporation, through the issuance and sale of shares.
Personnel	A collective term for all of the employees of an organization. Personnel is also commonly used to refer to the personnel management function or the organizational unit responsible for administering personnel programs.
Bond	Bond refers to a debt instrument, issued by a borrower and promising a specified stream of payments to the purchaser, usually regular interest payments plus a final repayment of principal.
Firm	An organization that employs resources to produce a good or service for profit and owns and operates one or more plants is referred to as a firm.
Profit	Profit refers to the return to the resource entrepreneurial ability; total revenue minus total cost.
Boot	Boot is any type of personal property received in a real property transaction that is not like kind, such as cash, mortgage notes, a boat or stock. The exchanger pays taxes on the boot to the extent of recognized capital gain. In an exchange if any funds are not used in purchasing the replacement property, that also will be called boot.
Divestiture	In finance and economics, divestiture is the reduction of some kind of asset, for either financial or social goals. A divestment is the opposite of an investment.
Organizational socialization	The process through which employees learn about the firm's culture and pass their knowledge and understanding on to others is called organizational socialization.
Preference	The act of a debtor in paying or securing one or more of his creditors in a manner more favorable to them than to other creditors or to the exclusion of such other creditors is a preference. In the absence of statute, a preference is perfectly good, but to be legal it must be bona fide, and not a mere subterfuge of the debtor to secure a future benefit to himself or to prevent the application of his property to his debts.

Matching	Matching refers to an accounting concept that establishes when expenses are recognized. Expenses are matched with the revenues they helped to generate and are recognized when those revenues are recognized.
Policy	Similar to a script in that a policy can be a less than completely rational decision-making method. Involves the use of a pre-existing set of decision steps for any problem that presents itself.
Sam Walton	I guess in all my years, what I heard more often than anything was: a town of less than 50,000 population cannot support a discount store for very long. Sam Walton was the founder of two American retailers, Wal-Mart and Sam's Club.
Deutsche Bank	Deutsche Bank was founded in Germany on January 22, 1870 as a specialist bank for foreign trade. Major projects in its first decades included the Northern Pacific Railroad in the United States (1883) and the Baghdad Railway (1888). It also financed bond offerings of the steel concern Krupp (1885) and introduced the chemical company Bayer on the Berlin stock market.
Operation	A standardized method or technique that is performed repetitively, often on different materials resulting in different finished goods is called an operation.
Novell	Novell is an American high-technology corporation specializing in network operating systems such as NetWare and Linux, secure identity management products, and application integration and collaboration solutions.
Alcoa	Alcoa (NYSE: AA) is the world's leading producer of alumina, primary and fabricated aluminum, with operations in 43 countries. (It is followed in this by a former subsidiary, Alcan, the second-leading producer.)
Common area	Common area is area on a piece of property or part of a building that is available for use to all owners or tenents. Examples include: hallways, swimming pools, parking garage, and cummunity centers.
Corporation	A legal entity chartered by a state or the Federal government that is distinct and separate from the individuals who own it is a corporation. This separation gives the corporation unique powers which other legal entities lack.
Economy	The income, expenditures, and resources that affect the cost of running a business and household are called an economy.
Attest	To bear witness to is called attest. To affirm, certify by oath or signature. It is an official act establishing authenticity.
Jargon	Jargon is terminology, much like slang, that relates to a specific activity, profession, or group. It develops as a kind of shorthand, to express ideas that are frequently discussed between members of a group, and can also have the effect of distinguishing those belonging to a group from those who are not.
Evaluation	The consumer's appraisal of the product or brand on important attributes is called evaluation.
Leadership	Management merely consists of leadership applied to business situations; or in other words: management forms a sub-set of the broader process of leadership.
Cultural values	The values that employees need to have and act on for the organization to act on the strategic values are called cultural values.
Shareholder	A shareholder is an individual or company (including a corporation) that legally owns one or more shares of stock in a joined stock company.
Senior	Senior management is generally a team of individuals at the highest level of organizational

management	management who have the day-to-day responsibilities of managing a corporation.
Code of ethics	A formal statement of ethical principles and rules of conduct is a code of ethics. Some may have the force of law; these are often promulgated by the (quasi-)governmental agency responsible for licensing a profession. Violations of these codes may be subject to administrative (e.g., loss of license), civil or penal remedies.
Ethical dilemma	An ethical dilemma is a situation that often involves an apparent conflict between moral imperatives, in which to obey one would result in transgressing another.
Standards of conduct	Standards of conduct refers to a compendium of ethical norms promulgated by an organization to guide the behavior of its members. Many government agencies have formal codes of conduct for their employees.
Walt Disney	As the co-founder of Walt Disney Productions, Walt became one of the most well-known motion picture producers in the world. The corporation he co-founded, now known as The Walt Disney Company, today has annual revenues of approximately US $30 billion.
Competitor	Other organizations in the same industry or type of business that provide a good or service to the same set of customers is referred to as a competitor.
Revenue	Revenue is a U.S. business term for the amount of money that a company receives from its activities, mostly from sales of products and/or services to customers.
Service	Service refers to a "non tangible product" that is not embodied in a physical good and that typically effects some change in another product, person, or institution. Contrasts with good.
Regulation	Regulation refers to restrictions state and federal laws place on business with regard to the conduct of its activities.
Option	A contract that gives the purchaser the option to buy or sell the underlying financial instrument at a specified price, called the exercise price or strike price, within a specific period of time.
Active listening	Active listening is a way of "listening for meaning" in which the listener checks with the speaker to see that a statement has been correctly heard and understood. The goal of active listening is to improve mutual understanding.
Customer service	The ability of logistics management to satisfy users in terms of time, dependability, communication, and convenience is called the customer service.
Incentive	An incentive is any factor (financial or non-financial) that provides a motive for a particular course of action, or counts as a reason for preferring one choice to the alternatives.
Southwest airlines	Southwest Airlines is a low-fare airline in the United States. It is the third-largest airline in the world, by number of passengers carried, and the largest in the United States by number of passengers carried domestically.
Context	The effect of the background under which a message often takes on more and richer meaning is a context. Context is especially important in cross-cultural interactions because some cultures are said to be high context or low context.
Organizational Behavior	The study of human behavior in organizational settings, the interface between human behavior and the organization, and the organization itself is called organizational behavior.
Household	An economic unit that provides the economy with resources and uses the income received to purchase goods and services that satisfy economic wants is called household.
Security	Security refers to a claim on the borrower future income that is sold by the borrower to the

lender. A security is a type of transferable interest representing financial value.

Downturn | A decline in a stock market or economic cycle is a downturn.

Attrition | The practice of not hiring new employees to replace older employees who either quit or retire is referred to as attrition.

Buyout | A buyout is an investment transaction by which the entire or a controlling part of the stock of a company is sold. A firm buysout the stake of the company to strengthen its influence on the company's decision making body. A buyout can take the forms of a leveraged buyout or a management buyout.

Openness | Openness refers to the extent to which an economy is open, often measured by the ratio of its trade to GDP.

Trust | An arrangement in which shareholders of independent firms agree to give up their stock in exchange for trust certificates that entitle them to a share of the trust's common profits.

Distribution | Distribution in economics, the manner in which total output and income is distributed among individuals or factors.

Empowerment | Giving employees the authority and responsibility to respond quickly to customer requests is called empowerment.

Employee empowerment | Employee empowerment is a method of improving customer service in which workers have discretion to do what they believe is necessary, but within reason, to satisfy the customer, even if this means bending some company rules.

Authority | Authority in agency law, refers to an agent's ability to affect his principal's legal relations with third parties. Also used to refer to an actor's legal power or ability to do something. In addition, sometimes used to refer to a statute, case, or other legal source that justifies a particular result.

Productivity | Productivity refers to the total output of goods and services in a given period of time divided by work hours.

Multinational corporation | An organization that manufactures and markets products in many different countries and has multinational stock ownership and multinational management is referred to as multinational corporation.

Paradox | As used in economics, paradox means something unexpected, rather than the more extreme normal meaning of something seemingly impossible. Some paradoxes are just theoretical results that go against what one thinks of as normal.

Balance | In banking and accountancy, the outstanding balance is the amount of money owned, (or due), that remains in a deposit account (or a loan account) at a given date, after all past remittances, payments and withdrawal have been accounted for. It can be positive (then, in the balance sheet of a firm, it is an asset) or negative (a liability).

Applicant	In many tribunal and administrative law suits, the person who initiates the claim is called the applicant.
Interpersonal skills	Interpersonal skills are used to communicate with, understand, and motivate individuals and groups.
Aptitude	An aptitude is an innate inborn ability to do a certain kind of work. Aptitudes may be physical or mental. Many of them have been identified and are testable.
Interest	In finance and economics, interest is the price paid by a borrower for the use of a lender's money. In other words, interest is the amount of paid to "rent" money for a period of time.
Employment test	A written or computerbased test designed to measure a particular attribute such as intelligence or aptitude is an employment test.
Complexity	The technical sophistication of the product and hence the amount of understanding required to use it is referred to as complexity. It is the opposite of simplicity.
Staffing	Staffing refers to a management function that includes hiring, motivating, and retaining the best people available to accomplish the company's objectives.
Toyota	Toyota is a Japanese multinational corporation that manufactures automobiles, trucks and buses. Toyota is the world's second largest automaker by sales. Toyota also provides financial services through its subsidiary, Toyota Financial Services, and participates in other lines of business.
Assessment center	Assessment center refers to a process in which multiple raters evaluate employees' performance on a number of exercises.
Assessment	Collecting information and providing feedback to employees about their behavior, communication style, or skills is an assessment.
Personnel	A collective term for all of the employees of an organization. Personnel is also commonly used to refer to the personnel management function or the organizational unit responsible for administering personnel programs.
Management	Management characterizes the process of leading and directing all or part of an organization, often a business, through the deployment and manipulation of resources. Early twentieth-century management writer Mary Parker Follett defined management as "the art of getting things done through people."
Personality test	A personality test aims to describe aspects of a person's character that remain stable throughout a person's lifetime. A model of personality were first posited by Greek philosopher/physician Hippocrates.
Corporation	A legal entity chartered by a state or the Federal government that is distinct and separate from the individuals who own it is a corporation. This separation gives the corporation unique powers which other legal entities lack.
Leadership	Management merely consists of leadership applied to business situations; or in other words: management forms a sub-set of the broader process of leadership.
Ethics training	Training programs to help employees deal with ethical questions and values are called ethics training.
Basic skills	Basic skills refer to reading, writing, and communication skills needed to understand the content of a training program.
Gap	In December of 1995, Gap became the first major North American retailer to accept independent monitoring of the working conditions in a contract factory producing its garments. Gap is the largest specialty retailer in the United States.

Firm	An organization that employs resources to produce a good or service for profit and owns and operates one or more plants is referred to as a firm.
Technology	The body of knowledge and techniques that can be used to combine economic resources to produce goods and services is called technology.
Organization design	The structuring of workers so that they can best accomplish the firm's goals is referred to as organization design.
Quality management	Quality management is a method for ensuring that all the activities necessary to design, develop and implement a product or service are effective and efficient with respect to the system and its performance.
Value system	A value system refers to how an individual or a group of individuals organize their ethical or ideological values. A well-defined value system is a moral code.
Trend	Trend refers to the long-term movement of an economic variable, such as its average rate of increase or decrease over enough years to encompass several business cycles.
Production line	A production line is a set of sequential operations established in a factory whereby materials are put through a refining process to produce an end-product that is suitable for onward consumption; or components are assembled to make a finished article.
Production	The creation of finished goods and services using the factors of production: land, labor, capital, entrepreneurship, and knowledge.
Siemens	Siemens is the world's largest conglomerate company. Worldwide, Siemens and its subsidiaries employs 461,000 people (2005) in 190 countries and reported global sales of €75.4 billion in fiscal year 2005.
Apprenticeship	A work-study training method with both on-the-job and classroom training is an apprenticeship.Most of their training is on the job, working for an employer who helps the apprentices learn their trade, art or craft. Less formal, theoretical education is involved.
Job rotation	A job enrichment strategy that involves moving employees from one job to another is a job rotation.
Assignment	A transfer of property or some right or interest is referred to as assignment.
Mentoring	Mentoring refers to a developmental relationship between a more experienced mentor and a less experienced partner referred to as a mentee or protégé. Usually - but not necessarily - the mentor/protégé pair will be of the same sex.
Operation	A standardized method or technique that is performed repetitively, often on different materials resulting in different finished goods is called an operation.
Loyalty	Marketers tend to define customer loyalty as making repeat purchases. Some argue that it should be defined attitudinally as a strongly positive feeling about the brand.
Promotion	Promotion refers to all the techniques sellers use to motivate people to buy products or services. An attempt by marketers to inform people about products and to persuade them to participate in an exchange.
Hierarchy	A system of grouping people in an organization according to rank from the top down in which all subordinate managers must report to one person is called a hierarchy.
Career planning	Process in which individuals evaluate their abilities and interests, consider alternative career opportunities, establish career goals, and plan practical development activities is referred to as career planning.
Small business	Small business refers to a business that is independently owned and operated, is not dominant in its field of operation, and meets certain standards of size in terms of employees or

	annual receipts.
Entrepreneur	The owner/operator. The person who organizes, manages, and assumes the risks of a firm, taking a new idea or a new product and turning it into a successful business is an entrepreneur.
Specialist	A specialist is a trader who makes a market in one or several stocks and holds the limit order book for those stocks.
Balance	In banking and accountancy, the outstanding balance is the amount of money owned, (or due), that remains in a deposit account (or a loan account) at a given date, after all past remittances, payments and withdrawal have been accounted for. It can be positive (then, in the balance sheet of a firm, it is an asset) or negative (a liability).
Industry	A group of firms that produce identical or similar products is an industry. It is also used specifically to refer to an area of economic production focused on manufacturing which involves large amounts of capital investment before any profit can be realized, also called "heavy industry".
Performance appraisal	An evaluation in which the performance level of employees is measured against established standards to make decisions about promotions, compenzation, additional training, or firing is referred to as performance appraisal.
Consultant	A professional that provides expert advice in a particular field or area in which customers occassionaly require this type of knowledge is a consultant.
Contribution	In business organization law, the cash or property contributed to a business by its owners is referred to as contribution.
Cooperative	A business owned and controlled by the people who use it, producers, consumers, or workers with similar needs who pool their resources for mutual gain is called cooperative.
Authority	Authority in agency law, refers to an agent's ability to affect his principal's legal relations with third parties. Also used to refer to an actor's legal power or ability to do something. In addition, sometimes used to refer to a statute, case, or other legal source that justifies a particular result.
Telecommuting	Telecommuting is a work arrangement in which employees enjoy limited flexibility in working location and hours.
Evaluation	The consumer's appraisal of the product or brand on important attributes is called evaluation.
Comprehensive	A comprehensive refers to a layout accurate in size, color, scheme, and other necessary details to show how a final ad will look. For presentation only, never for reproduction.
Empowerment	Giving employees the authority and responsibility to respond quickly to customer requests is called empowerment.
Internal customer	An individuals or unit within the firm that receives services from other entities within the organization is an internal customer.
DuPont	DuPont was the inventor of CFCs (along with General Motors) and the largest producer of these ozone depleting chemicals (used primarily in aerosol sprays and refrigerants) in the world, with a 25% market share in the late 1980s.
Sprint	The Sprint Corporation was founded in 1899 by Cleyson Leroy Brown under the name of the "Brown Telephone Company" in the small town of Abilene, Kansas. The company was a landline telephone company that operated as a competitor to the Bell System.
Alcoa	Alcoa (NYSE: AA) is the world's leading producer of alumina, primary and fabricated aluminum,

	with operations in 43 countries. (It is followed in this by a former subsidiary, Alcan, the second-leading producer.)
Gain	In finance, gain is a profit or an increase in value of an investment such as a stock or bond. Gain is calculated by fair market value or the proceeds from the sale of the investment minus the sum of the purchase price and all costs associated with it.
Graphic rating scale	A scale that lists a variety of dimensions thought to be related to high performance outcomes in a given job and that one is expected to exhibit is referred to as the graphic rating scale.
Behaviorally Anchored Rating Scale	A performance appraisal approach that describes observable job behaviors, each of which is evaluated to determine good versus bad performance is referred to as behaviorally anchored rating scale.
Performance behaviors	The total set of work-related behaviors that the organization expects the individual to display are referred to as performance behaviors.
Halo error	That which results when one person rates another person on several different dimensions and gives a similar rating for each one is halo error.
Supervisor	A Supervisor is an employee of an organization with some of the powers and responsibilities of management, occupying a role between true manager and a regular employee. A Supervisor position is typically the first step towards being promoted into a management role.
Discount	The difference between the face value of a bond and its selling price, when a bond is sold for less than its face value it's referred to as a discount.
Due process	Due process of law is a legal concept that ensures the government will respect all of a person's legal rights instead of just some or most of those legal rights when the government deprives a person of life, liberty, or property.
Hearing	A hearing is a proceeding before a court or other decision-making body or officer. A hearing is generally distinguished from a trial in that it is usually shorter and often less formal.
Performance feedback	The process of providing employees with information regarding their performance effectiveness is referred to as performance feedback.
Bill Gates	Bill Gates is the co-founder, chairman, former chief software architect, and former CEO of Microsoft Corporation. He is one of the best-known entrepreneurs of the personal computer revolution and he is widely respected for his foresight and ambition.
Microsoft	Microsoft is a multinational computer technology corporation with 2004 global annual sales of US$39.79 billion and 71,553 employees in 102 countries and regions as of July 2006. It develops, manufactures, licenses, and supports a wide range of software products for computing devices.
Users	Users refer to people in the organization who actually use the product or service purchased by the buying center.
Context	The effect of the background under which a message often takes on more and richer meaning is a context. Context is especially important in cross-cultural interactions because some cultures are said to be high context or low context.
Time orientation	The extent to which members of a culture adopt a long term versus a short term outlook on work is time orientation.
Points	Loan origination fees that may be deductible as interest by a buyer of property. A seller of property who pays points reduces the selling price by the amount of the points paid for the buyer.

Training and development	All attempts to improve productivity by increasing an employee's ability to perform is training and development.

Policy	Similar to a script in that a policy can be a less than completely rational decision-making method. Involves the use of a pre-existing set of decision steps for any problem that presents itself.
Industry	A group of firms that produce identical or similar products is an industry. It is also used specifically to refer to an area of economic production focused on manufacturing which involves large amounts of capital investment before any profit can be realized, also called "heavy industry".
Consolidation	The combination of two or more firms, generally of equal size and market power, to form an entirely new entity is a consolidation.
Competitor	Other organizations in the same industry or type of business that provide a good or service to the same set of customers is referred to as a competitor.
Escalation	Regarding the structure of tariffs. In the context of a trade war, escalation refers to the increase in tariffs that occurs as countries retaliate again and again.
Interest	In finance and economics, interest is the price paid by a borrower for the use of a lender's money. In other words, interest is the amount of paid to "rent" money for a period of time.
Economy	The income, expenditures, and resources that affect the cost of running a business and household are called an economy.
Merger	Merger refers to the combination of two firms into a single firm.
Market	A market is, as defined in economics, a social arrangement that allows buyers and sellers to discover information and carry out a voluntary exchange of goods or services.
Firm	An organization that employs resources to produce a good or service for profit and owns and operates one or more plants is referred to as a firm.
Service	Service refers to a "non tangible product" that is not embodied in a physical good and that typically effects some change in another product, person, or institution. Contrasts with good.
Globalization	The increasing world-wide integration of markets for goods, services and capital that attracted special attention in the late 1990s is called globalization.
Security	Security refers to a claim on the borrower future income that is sold by the borrower to the lender. A security is a type of transferable interest representing financial value.
Change agent	A change agent is someone who engages either deliberately or whose behavior results in social, cultural or behavioral change. This can be studied scientifically and effective techniques can be discovered and employed.
Consultant	A professional that provides expert advice in a particular field or area in which customers occassionaly require this type of knowledge is a consultant.
Agent	A person who makes economic decisions for another economic actor. A hired manager operates as an agent for a firm's owner.
Personnel	A collective term for all of the employees of an organization. Personnel is also commonly used to refer to the personnel management function or the organizational unit responsible for administering personnel programs.
Specialist	A specialist is a trader who makes a market in one or several stocks and holds the limit order book for those stocks.
Status quo	Status quo is a Latin term meaning the present, current, existing state of affairs.
Frequency	Frequency refers to the speed of the up and down movements of a fluctuating economic

	variable; that is, the number of times per unit of time that the variable completes a cycle of up and down movement.
Unfreezing	The process by which people become aware of the need for change is unfreezing.
Refreezing	The process of making new behaviors relatively permanent and resistant to further change is refreezing.
Organizational Behavior	The study of human behavior in organizational settings, the interface between human behavior and the organization, and the organization itself is called organizational behavior.
Resistance to change	Resistance to change refers to an attitude or behavior that shows unwillingness to make or support a change.
Management	Management characterizes the process of leading and directing all or part of an organization, often a business, through the deployment and manipulation of resources. Early twentieth-century management writer Mary Parker Follett defined management as "the art of getting things done through people."
Loyalty	Marketers tend to define customer loyalty as making repeat purchases. Some argue that it should be defined attitudinally as a strongly positive feeling about the brand.
Mistake	In contract law a mistake is incorrect understanding by one or more parties to a contract and may be used as grounds to invalidate the agreement. Common law has identified three different types of mistake in contract: unilateral mistake, mutual mistake, and common mistake.
Accumulation	The acquisition of an increasing quantity of something. The accumulation of factors, especially capital, is a primary mechanism for economic growth.
Complexity	The technical sophistication of the product and hence the amount of understanding required to use it is referred to as complexity. It is the opposite of simplicity.
Boeing	Boeing is the world's largest aircraft manufacturer by revenue. Headquartered in Chicago, Illinois, Boeing is the second-largest defense contractor in the world. In 2005, the company was the world's largest civil aircraft manufacturer in terms of value.
Ford	Ford is an American company that manufactures and sells automobiles worldwide. Ford introduced methods for large-scale manufacturing of cars, and large-scale management of an industrial workforce, especially elaborately engineered manufacturing sequences typified by the moving assembly lines.
Productivity	Productivity refers to the total output of goods and services in a given period of time divided by work hours.
Statistical process control	Statistical process control is a method for achieving quality control in manufacturing processes. It is a set of methods using statistical tools such as mean, variance and others, to detect whether the process observed is under control.
Quality management	Quality management is a method for ensuring that all the activities necessary to design, develop and implement a product or service are effective and efficient with respect to the system and its performance.
Production	The creation of finished goods and services using the factors of production: land, labor, capital, entrepreneurship, and knowledge.
Argument	The discussion by counsel for the respective parties of their contentions on the law and the facts of the case being tried in order to aid the jury in arriving at a correct and just conclusion is called argument.
Socialization	Socialization is the process by which human beings or animals learn to adopt the behavior patterns of the community in which they live. For both humans and animals, this is typically

	thought to occur during the early stages of life, during which individuals develop the skills and knowledge necessary to function within their culture and environment.
Union	A worker association that bargains with employers over wages and working conditions is called a union.
Administration	Administration refers to the management and direction of the affairs of governments and institutions; a collective term for all policymaking officials of a government; the execution and implementation of public policy.
Outsourcing	Outsourcing refers to a production activity that was previously done inside a firm or plant that is now conducted outside that firm or plant.
Authority	Authority in agency law, refers to an agent's ability to affect his principal's legal relations with third parties. Also used to refer to an actor's legal power or ability to do something. In addition, sometimes used to refer to a statute, case, or other legal source that justifies a particular result.
Resource allocation	Resource allocation refers to the manner in which an economy distributes its resources among the potential uses so as to produce a particular set of final goods.
Allocation of resources	Allocation of resources refers to the society's decisions on how to divide up its scarce input resources among the different outputs produced in the economy, and among the different firms or other organizations that produce those outputs.
Credibility	The extent to which a source is perceived as having knowledge, skill, or experience relevant to a communication topic and can be trusted to give an unbiased opinion or present objective information on the issue is called credibility.
Trust	An arrangement in which shareholders of independent firms agree to give up their stock in exchange for trust certificates that entitle them to a share of the trust's common profits.
Contribution	In business organization law, the cash or property contributed to a business by its owners is referred to as contribution.
Active listening	Active listening is a way of "listening for meaning" in which the listener checks with the speaker to see that a statement has been correctly heard and understood. The goal of active listening is to improve mutual understanding.
Empathy	Empathy refers to dimension of service quality-caring individualized attention provided to customers.
Openness	Openness refers to the extent to which an economy is open, often measured by the ratio of its trade to GDP.
Organizational development	The application of behavioral science knowledge in a longrange effort to improve an organization's ability to cope with change in its external environment and increase its problem-solving capabilities is referred to as organizational development.
Collaboration	Collaboration occurs when the interaction between groups is very important to goal attainment and the goals are compatible. Wherein people work together —applying both to the work of individuals as well as larger collectives and societies.
Coercion	Economic coercion is when an agent puts economic pressure onto the victim. The most common example of this is cutting off the supply to an essential resource, such as water.
Conflict resolution	Conflict resolution is the process of resolving a dispute or a conflict. Successful conflict resolution occurs by providing each side's needs, and adequately addressing their interests so that they are each satisfied with the outcome. Conflict resolution aims to end conflicts before they start or lead to physical fighting.

Supervisor	A Supervisor is an employee of an organization with some of the powers and responsibilities of management, occupying a role between true manager and a regular employee. A Supervisor position is typically the first step towards being promoted into a management role.
Process consultation	Process consultation involves interviewing people and observing work group processes to uncover interpersonal stumbling blocks and related problems. A change agent will then provide feedback aimed at improving the work process.
Formal communication channel	Formal communication channel refers to a communication channel that flows within the chain of command or task responsibility defined by the organization.
Channel	Channel, in communications (sometimes called communications channel), refers to the medium used to convey information from a sender (or transmitter) to a receiver.
Communication channel	The pathways through which messages are communicated are called a communication channel.
Action plan	Action plan refers to a written document that includes the steps the trainee and manager will take to ensure that training transfers to the job.
Team building	A term that describes the process of identifying roles for team members and helping the team members succeed in their roles is called team building.
Dysfunctional conflict	Conflict that is responsible for hindering group performance is dysfunctional conflict.
Disparity	Disparity refers to the regional and economic differences in a country, province, state, or continent
Integration	Economic integration refers to reducing barriers among countries to transactions and to movements of goods, capital, and labor, including harmonization of laws, regulations, and standards. Integrated markets theoretically function as a unified market.
Avon	Avon is an American cosmetics, perfume and toy seller with markets in over 135 countries across the world and a sales of $7.74 billion worldwide.
Futures	Futures refer to contracts for the sale and future delivery of stocks or commodities, wherein either party may waive delivery, and receive or pay, as the case may be, the difference in market price at the time set for delivery.
Technology	The body of knowledge and techniques that can be used to combine economic resources to produce goods and services is called technology.
Continuous improvement	The constant effort to eliminate waste, reduce response time, simplify the design of both products and processes, and improve quality and customer service is referred to as continuous improvement.
Customer satisfaction	Customer satisfaction is a business term which is used to capture the idea of measuring how satisfied an enterprise's customers are with the organization's efforts in a marketplace.
Continuous process	An uninterrupted production process in which long production runs turn out finished goods over time is called continuous process.
Process improvement	Process improvement is the activity of elevating the performance of a process, especially that of a business process with regard to its goal.
Reengineering	The fundamental rethinking and redesign of business processes to achieve improvements in critical measures of performance, such as cost, quality, service, speed, and customer satisfaction is referred to as reengineering.
Process	Process reengineering refers to the total rethinking and redesign of organizational process

reengineering	to improve performance and innovation; involves analyzing, streamlining, and reconfiguring actions and tasks to achieve work goals.
Operation	A standardized method or technique that is performed repetitively, often on different materials resulting in different finished goods is called an operation.
Core	A core is the set of feasible allocations in an economy that cannot be improved upon by subset of the set of the economy's consumers (a coalition). In construction, when the force in an element is within a certain center section, the core, the element will only be under compression.
Comprehensive	A comprehensive refers to a layout accurate in size, color, scheme, and other necessary details to show how a final ad will look. For presentation only, never for reproduction.
Strategic planning	The process of determining the major goals of the organization and the policies and strategies for obtaining and using resources to achieve those goals is called strategic planning.
Middle management	Middle management refers to the level of management that includes general managers, division managers, and branch and plant managers who are responsible for tactical planning and controlling.
Downsizing	The process of eliminating managerial and non-managerial positions are called downsizing.
Promotion	Promotion refers to all the techniques sellers use to motivate people to buy products or services. An attempt by marketers to inform people about products and to persuade them to participate in an exchange.
Consumption	In Keynesian economics consumption refers to personal consumption expenditure, i.e., the purchase of currently produced goods and services out of income, out of savings (net worth), or from borrowed funds. It refers to that part of disposable income that does not go to saving.
Turnover	Turnover in a financial context refers to the rate at which a provider of goods cycles through its average inventory. Turnover in a human resources context refers to the characteristic of a given company or industry, relative to rate at which an employer gains and loses staff.
Organizational communication	Thee process by which information is exchanged in the organizational setting is organizational communication.
Gain	In finance, gain is a profit or an increase in value of an investment such as a stock or bond. Gain is calculated by fair market value or the proceeds from the sale of the investment minus the sum of the purchase price and all costs associated with it.
Corporation	A legal entity chartered by a state or the Federal government that is distinct and separate from the individuals who own it is a corporation. This separation gives the corporation unique powers which other legal entities lack.
Innovation	Innovation refers to the first commercially successful introduction of a new product, the use of a new method of production, or the creation of a new form of business organization.
Variable	A variable is something measured by a number; it is used to analyze what happens to other things when the size of that number changes.
Vertical differentiation	Vertical differentiation refers to the centralization and decentralization of decision-making responsibilities.
Centralization	A structural policy in which decision-making authority is concentrated at the top of the organizational hierarchy is referred to as centralization.

Adoption	In corporation law, a corporation's acceptance of a pre-incorporation contract by action of its board of directors, by which the corporation becomes liable on the contract, is referred to as adoption.
Organic organization	A term created by Tom Burns and G.M. Stalker in the late 1950s, an organic organization is an organization which is flexible and values outside knowledge.
Leadership	Management merely consists of leadership applied to business situations; or in other words: management forms a sub-set of the broader process of leadership.
Organizational design	The structuring of workers so that they can best accomplish the firm's goals is referred to as organizational design.

Printed in the United States
68664LVS00003B/65-68

9 781428 811577